Essays on
THE FOUNDATIONS OF ASTROLOGY

Essays on

THE FOUNDATIONS OF ASTROLOGY

By
CHARLES E. O. CARTER

ASTROLOGY CLASSICS
207 VICTORY LANE, BEL AIR MD 21014

On the cover: Foundations of a park in Lawrence,
November, 1972. Photograph by David R. Roell

*Photo of Charles Carter found in the 1972 printing of
Astrological Aspects*

ISBN 978 1 933303 32 1

This edition published 2010

Published by
Astrology Classics

the publication division of
The Astrology Center of America
207 Victory Lane, Bel Air MD 21014

on line at www.**AstroAmerica.com**

CONTENTS

FOREWORD

This work was written during the war years.

It is hoped that it may contain some ideas that are worth preserving and possess novelty, although much that it contains will necessarily be reminiscent of what has appeared in my earlier works.

CHARLES E. O. CARTER.

1947

CHAPTER I

THE SUN, MOON AND MINOR PLANETS

To the ancients there were, of course, seven planets. That agreed admirably with, and perhaps was the origin and prime example of, the septenary principle they loved so well. The seven were the Sun, the Moon, Mercury, Venus, Mars, Jupiter and Saturn. The first two they call respectively the Greater and Lesser Luminaries. Mercury was a sort of odd man out ; he was the messenger of the gods, changeable by nature and accepting the value of whatever other planet or planets with which he might be in close aspect. Then came Venus and Jupiter, respectively the Lesser and Greater Benefics, naturally disposed to goodness in morals and to success and happiness ; and lastly Mars and Saturn were the Lesser and Greater Malefics, indicative of evil habits and dispositions and of difficult circumstances.

This scheme, simple and well-balanced, seemed to the medieval mind self-evidently true. In the arrangement of opposed good and evil planets, each considered as being ruled by an angel or archangel with innumerable subordinated spiritual beings, we seem to see a clear trace of Zoroastrian thought. The benefics are the servants of Ormuzd, the malefics are the agents of Ahriman.

The discovery of Copernicus shook this conception somewhat, but without very good reasons. Whether earth revolve round sun or sun round earth, the earth is still the centre of the universe for man and for all other inhabitants of earth. The sun itself is, so far as we know, only the centre of its own system ; it is not the centre of the cosmos.

Certainly the sun could no longer be regarded as a planet. But actually it had never been denied a

9

pre-eminent place in the scheme, even if it were so to speak but first amongst its equals.

A more serious blow was struck against astrology when Uranus, Neptune and Pluto were discovered.

In the old system the Luminaries and planets were each said to rule, or have a special affinity with, certain signs. Here, too, the allocation followed a regular pattern. The Sun and Moon respectively ruled Leo and Cancer, and then each planet, in the order of apparent motion, ruled two signs, thus :

	Leo		Cancer	
	Sun		*Moon*	
Virgo		*Mercury*		Gemini
Libra		*Venus*		Taurus
Scorpio		*Mars*		Aries
Sagittarius		*Jupiter*		Pisces
Capricorn		*Saturn*		Aquarius

It will be seen that the order of the signs is preserved, beginning with Aries and passing anti-clockwise from it to Pisces.

When other planets were discovered astrologers were placed in an awkward position. Some took up the stand that there was no reason to believe that the ancient ruler-ships would remain valid for all time. They might be subject to an evolutionary process. Finally there might be twelve known planets, one for each sign.* Uranus was said to be in process of supplanting Saturn from the rulership of Aquarius ; Neptune similarly seemed fitted, both by name and nature, to assume lordship over Pisces,

---

*It is interesting to note that there was an ancient allocation, preserved by Manilius, of the twelve signs to the Twelve Great Gods. In this Aries is ruled by Minerva, Gemini by Apollo, Cancer by Mercury, Leo by Jupiter, Virgo by Ceres, Libra by Vulcan, Sagittarius by Diana, Capricorn by Vesta, Aquarius by Juno, and Pisces by Neptune. Taurus and Scorpio are unchanged.

and Pluto suggested, again in name and in nature, the sign Scorpio.

Others remained loyal to the old scheme and only allowed the newly found bodies to have an "affinity" with certain signs. Perhaps they might, in the course of time, be found to have become their rulers, in the full sense, but practical experience did not, in their belief, as yet confirm their titles.

It is easy to see that there is a close correspondence between the definite and closed scheme of the medievalists and the general intellectual attitude of the times, as also between the present uncertain condition of astrological thought, in this regard, and the general confusionism of our own days.

But the notion that the discovery of the " new " planets had " disproved " astrology is ridiculous, and, when made by those who have not studied the subject—it is made by none others—it is equally presumptuous. The readiness to receive new factors is rather to the credit of astrologers than to their discredit and it would be well for mankind if all organised bodies of thought had shown a like alacrity to accept new discoveries.

It is the misfortune of astrology—if truth in any form can be unfortunate—that even when it has been examined by brilliant intellects it has usually been studied only superficially ; and minds normally free from prejudice have apparently forgotten this virtue when engaged upon the subject. Even Plotinus misunderstood when he condemned astrologers for speaking as if the planets, which the philosopher doubtless regarded as divine and therefore immutable, changed their natures. No astrologer has made any such assertion ; but it is true that planets are said to be well or badly placed according to their own mutual relations or aspects and the signs through which their values are translated to us. In essence they remain unchanged.

Thus planets were said to be well placed when in the signs they rule and in other signs denominated the signs of their " exaltation " ; and just as the planets themselves were divided into benefics and malefics, so the aspects were strictly classed as good and bad.

In modern times the terms benefic and malefic are not in such frequent use as formerly, and when they are employed, it is chiefly for brevity's sake. We shall consider later the appropriateness or otherwise of classing aspects as good and bad.

Another term that has brought attacks upon astrology is that of " influence " as applied to the planets, as also our speaking of their " effects." Moralists appear to dislike these expressions because they are supposed to imply fatalism, although it is undeniable that human life is subject to many influences and effects, as for example those of climate. No one is called a fatalist because he affirms that his rheumatism is worse when he lives on a clay subsoil ! Scientists laugh at " influences " which we cannot test by means of instruments (as if our own bodies and lives were not very delicate instruments !) but they themselves talk of many forces, such as gravitation, of the true nature of which they are themselves in doubt or in absolute ignorance.

Influence and effects are convenient words to use, but they are misleading. We assert only, as Kepler did, a *concurrence* of celestial and terrestrial conditions, and do not, for ourselves, venture further.

Having written of these more general matters, we will pass now to a consideration of the values of the members of our Solar System. The fixed stars are taken into account by some astrologers but not by any means by all, and we omit them from our present exposition.

THE SUN AND MOON, OR LUMINARIES

We have said that even to the old astrologers, with their Ptolemaic astronomy, the Sun was always something more than an ordinary planet. It is indeed the astrological symbol of the vital urge, the *élan vital*, life itself, indicating by its horoscopic position where the impulse to self-expression will manifest itself, with what intensity, and with what success. A well-aspected and well-sited Sun denotes a vital current that will flow steadily forward ; the reverse conditions point to a current which, to use metaphor, will be checked and broken by many rocks. Not that an afflicted Sun, even one severely afflicted in a technical sense, necessarily betokens a failure in life, for horoscopic conditions which would be regarded by most astrologers as in a certain sense very evil do often generate great strength, as if by reactional stimulus ; but the life would inevitably encounter many difficulties and obstacles to self-expression. What is commonly looked upon as a failure in life is usually indicated not so much by heavy afflictions in a technical sense, as by a map of poor integration, with few aspects of any kind.

The Twelve Labours of Hercules may be thought of as a solar myth with a direct application to human life. The Labours may be correlated with the special life-problems, exterior and interior, of each sign.

Exteriorly solar aspects usually express themselves in terms of physical well-being, i.e., health and liability or otherwise to accidents. In some cases there may seem to be little or no responsibility, so far as the native is concerned, for these : good or ill health may be inherited and the accidents may be due to no carelessness on his part. In other cases the reverse may be the case, and only a study of the figure of birth as a whole will reveal whether the subject is likely to be foolish, or unlucky, prudent or merely fortunate. Or, most often, something of both.

It would almost seem as if, from the point of view of the astrological agents—we write, of course, figuratively—it is a matter of indifference whether the appropriate conditions come into our lives by our own acts or from without, so long as they appear. But from a practical point of view we shall usually find that the positive type of map tends to lack prudence when afflictive conditions appear in the geniture and thus brings trouble upon itself, whilst the more Saturnian types exercise care as regards their own acts but may suffer from those of other people. For example, in war-time Britain the citizen was constantly affected in his personal life by things beyond his control, as by the requisitioning of houses.   There seems no reason to believe that such occurrences, over which one has no control, are less closely correlated with horoscopic conditions than are purely voluntary ones.

But, to return to the Sun, it does throw light upon the disposition. Although, as we have said, the Sun symbolises the impulse towards active life in a general sense, it has a predominantly emotional bias. It is, when well placed, indicative of emotional warmth, affection, love, large-heartedness and open and generous feelings.

Such characteristics will be most in evidence when the Sun occupies its own sign Leo, and without adverse planetary contacts, and with a congenial sign, perhaps Leo itself, on the eastern horizon.

Reverse horoscopic features point to a warping of the affectional nature, in the thousand and one ways and degrees which astrological symbology is capable of expressing. Yet, so powerful is the Sun in comparison with other bodies, these should not be overstressed in actual interpretation. It does not suffer to the extent that the Moon may do from planetary afflictions, at least in terms of character.

The Sun is also important in relation to the mind and intellectual powers, if it is in contact with an appropriate planet or in an intellectual sign, and this by reason of its vivifying power.   Since Mercury and Jupiter are preeminently the mental planets, as rulers of the four " common " or mental signs, an aspect to these bodies or either of them from the Sun invigorates the mind.

Furthermore, the Sun has a near relation to the will and the conative element in man, and the life of action, so that good or bad solar affects bear strongly upon the course of the career, both as regards its specific nature and the ease or difficulty with which the psyche is able to express itself in this field.

The moral nature, or sense of right and wrong, must not be judged from the Sun, or at least by no means wholly. Hitler's Sun was without technical affliction, that of Mussolini showed little to justify a cruel, licentious and treacherous nature.

Altogether the solar value is an outgoing one, masculine and positive.   With the Moon it forms the basic psychological polarity, of which the most obvious externalisation is in sex.   Hence these two bodies ought always to be considered together, the one furnishing the complementary value to the other.   The one is always the getter and giver, the other the keeper and preserver.   The Sun tends upwards and outwards, and forwards in time, the Moon draws downwards and inwards, and looks backwards to the past.   The Sun is bold and adventurous, the Moon prudent and traditional.   The Sun unfolds, the Moon infolds.   The Sun has faith ; the Moon likes tried ways, or, in certain conditions, has a propensity to superstition.

The Sun forms new habits, consciously and by the action of the will ; the Moon has relation to our prejudices, family observances and traditions, and if it does strike out for itself, does so carefully and shrewdly.   Under affliction the Moon, through the channels we have just mentioned, affects the moral nature according to the nature of the stress, Mars distorting the more physical instincts, while Saturn narrows and hardens, and so forth. Here, to refer again to the dictators, Mussolini had the Moon besieged between these two bodies, whilst Hitler, though his Moon had no bad aspect, was in its " fall " and in conjunction with Jupiter, which in turn was in its " detriment." The result was a severe conflict between the expansive action of Jupiter and the hardening of the personality caused by the Saturnian sign.

In their most external manifestations the Sun denotes powerful, rich and perhaps most of all well-born people, royalty and nobility, whereas the Moon is said to be the significatrix of the common people.

The Moon does not invigorate the bodies with which it is in contact as the Sun does, yet a lunar contact adds much to the importance of the body contacted and affects its values in lunar terms.

There is an unmistakable correspondence between the two Luminaries (or Lights as they are sometimes named) and the parents. This must not be pushed too far. It often happens, in practical horoscopy, that an afflicted Sun or Moon reflects the fortunes or character of the father or mother, but probably only insofar as the native himself is affected, exteriorly or interiorly, by them. For the children of the same parents often have their Luminaries very differently conditioned.

The Sun, however, has a clear relation to one's children, as expressions of one's physical and emotional life, and afflictions to the Sun, or in Leo, frequently exhibit themselves in this field. Thus, the Sun in difficult relation to Saturn, or Saturn in Leo, often denies children or at best limits their number and denotes an appropriate limitation to their self-expression. The former condition, in the maps of females, is frequently an indication of lifelong virginity.

Owing to the vital exuberance of a strong Sun, there is often a love of enjoyment and pleasure of many kinds, whereas the Moon husbands its resources and prefers a domestic sphere of activity.

Between these two, then, as the primary—but not the only—representatives of the active and passive poles of human nature, our whole life-expression oscillates. In a certain sense each is more important than the other. The Sun controls the chief decisions, the outstanding events and eminent achievements of our life, but the Moon, for the most part pedestrian and prosaic, is a much truer index of what we usually are and are seen to be. The Sun is the height we may attain ; the Moon is our habitual level. Similarly the solar afflictions indicate great and permanent inhibitions ; the lunar, day-by-day frictions.

Around this soli-lunar axis, as it were, there is the constant interplay of the planetary motions, each with its own significance. The whole dramatic action is seen through the media of the Twelve Signs, and a further modification is affected, as we shall see, by the Mundane Houses.

Before we leave the subject of the Sun, however, we may mention the subject of heliocentric astrology.

If it be true doctrine that all astrological values within the solar system originate from the Sun, if not as actual " influences " at any rate symbolically, then the conditions operative (again actually or symbolically) at the Sun must possess some value even for beings resident on the earth. Aspects can be formed, of course, at the Sun. If then Mars and Jupiter, for example, are in trine at the Sun when " A " is born but in square when " B " begins his earthly existence, it does not seem unreasonable to suppose that these circumstances may affect the values of these three bodies in both nativities, inclining them to harmonious action in " A's " case, and to discordant operation in that of " B." This point does not seem unworthy of consideration.

When astrologers go so far as to insert heliocentric positions in a terrestrial horoscope and even take aspects from these to the ordinary geocentric places of planets, the practice seems less reasonable and to call for a very critical examination.

MERCURY

The basic idea or value of this planet may perhaps be adequately stated as the imparting and communication of knowledge and information. It is fundamentally mental and rules two mental or " common " signs. Mythology is not always a clear guide to astrological doctrine but often it throws a brilliant light upon our science. Hermes was the messenger of the Gods ; he was also a god of commerce, the word Mercury being related to *merces*, meaning gain, trade or profit. He invented the lyre, which recalls the inventive abilities of Virgo ; he conducted the souls of the departed to the nether world.

The nervous system is ruled by Mercury and in particular the senses. Speech, and the written word, come under him and all activities that serve the intercommunication of thought, such as the press, the postal service, and teaching.

He tends to precision and exactitude and has but little relation with the emotions or the will, but all physical things that are subservient to the transfer of ideas are ruled by him, and he has a concrete expression in travel, tradition emphasising that his rulership extends only to short journeys, and those which are not so much exploratory as routine matters—trips to and fro. Vehicles that serve this purpose, such as bicycles, trams and buses, come under him.

The Mercurial is usually good with his hands and fingers,

and he is often mechanical, working in wood or metal according to other contributory factors in the individual horoscope.

Here we find a kinship with the idea of Vulcan, or the Divine Smith, though the Virginian is usually fonder of delicate work, such as clock-making, than of the more strenuous forms of handicraft. The Vulcan-conception must be taken to include a strong Scorpio element, as well as Virgo. It is to be noted nevertheless that lameness is very often shown by a Virgo affliction, and that Virgo and Scorpio were at one time united, Libra being absent, according to an ancient legend, preserved by Virgil.

Through the negative sign Virgo he is often interested in horticulture, but it is possible that the asteroid Ceres may enter into this aspect of his activity. It has, indeed, been suggested that Virgo is actually ruled by the plane-toids, of which the four largest are named Ceres, Pallas, Juno and Vesta. With the exception of Juno these seem to have a Virginian relationship.

It has been stated that Mercury is an index to the moral nature. In itself the planet, like mind, is amoral and some-what detached and selfish. When severely afflicted it tends to a reckless or self-seeking use of the intellect and some-times to cruelty. Mythology portrays the god as a thief, whose cleverness, however, was often such as to amuse the victim rather than anger him. Thus Horace writes (Carminum Lib. I, 10) : " Apollo could not but laugh when, as he threatened to punish the boy (Mercury) for having stolen his oxen, he found that meantime he had emptied his quiver."

Thieving, in all its forms, is still related to an afflicted Mercury and there is still, in many of the children of the planet, a certain freshness and impudence that is not with-out its disarming aspects. Gemini, in particular, is a sign that is often endowed with a certain youthfulness even when the native is advanced in years, for the mind grows old less certainly than the body.

Besides dishonesty, a heavily afflicted Mercury may indicate a danger of mental instability ; but in this case there are other points to be considered.

It must not be thought that the mental powers can be judged only from this planet. It is true that a well-placed Mercury points to a quick brain, ready self-expression, fluency and mental agility, but it is a matter of the expression of intelligence rather than intelligence itself. Very learned persons may have Mercury by no means particularly well placed, as for example Einstein (Mercury in close conjunction with Saturn, in Aries, otherwise no strong contacts).

A strong Mercury does, however, usually indicate common-sense and a good judgment in practical matters.

Through Virgo the planet is also related to health, medicine, especially of the herbal school, and to physical culture. This is also mentioned by Horace in the ode cited above, where the god is said to have civilised man, " being skilled in voice and in the way of the graceful palaestra," or gymnasium.

In contrast with Venus, Mercury is analytical and inclined to see differences, whereas Venus conciliates. In contrast with the ruler of the two other mental signs, Jupiter, there is something of the same distinction, Jupiter being critical always with a view to final integration or at least to improvement. Mercury is without the hopefulness of the Great Benefic, being factual and " down to brass tacks," though, as we have said, not without a remedial aspect. He is mobile and often superficial and obvious, whereas Saturn is steady and often profound. He is without the drastic quality of Uranus, with whom he has nevertheless much in common. He has least affinity with Mars, whose contacts invigorate but often overstrain his powers. Neptune appears to render him, so to say, impish and irresponsible, but often charming, witty or humorous, as in the case of G. B. Shaw (Mercury in close trine to Neptune in Water). Solar affects tend to dogmatism and intellectual pride. The Moon with Mercury makes the mind shrewd and well able to deal with practical, everyday affairs, but it introduces an element of prejudice and parochialism.

VENUS

Venus is the planet of collaboration and the perception of resemblances. In this sense it is operative emotionally, mentally and in exterior activities. It tends always to see points of likeness and common interests and to gloss over or remove differences. It is gregarious and social. It is also characterised by a keen sense of probity and justice, inasmuch as dishonesty and injustice destroy the possibility of harmonious collaboration. It enters into every human activity that involves unification of feeling, thought or effort.

It is easy, therefore, to see why it has been denominated a benefic planet, and how the adage has arisen that " Venus harms no one." Naturally, since co-operation is most securely founded upon common interests, whether these be ideal or self-seeking, Venus cannot, in her essence, harm others, because that is contrary to her innermost characteristic. But that does not mean that a complex in which the planet is involved may not indicate serious difficulties.   It cannot be overstressed that a planet very rarely presents in a horoscope a pure value. Such a formation as Venus unaspected in Taurus in the 2nd house, or in Libra in the 7th, would come as near to this as possible. But even in these cases, though the planet is unaspected, its value inheres in a total horoscope and is translated to the individual through this *coelum*. Much more commonly a planet is neither in its own house nor sign and is implicated in more than one planetary formation.

In such circumstances Venus still remains a conciliatory value, and the tendency is towards construction rather than destruction. One sees this, for example, in the case of Hitler, born under Libra with the Sun in Taurus. Venus is terribly afflicted but there is still the ideal, however repellent to most non-Germans, of a New Order, and also a love of architecture.

Although pure examples rarely occur in practice, there are, theoretically, three degrees of intensity in which a planetary value may appear in the horoscope. It may be excessive, deficient, or normal. And apart from intensity, it may indicate constructive or harmonious manifestation, or the opposite.

In the case of Hitler, the Venus-value was in excess of balance and suffered a terrible distortion from the conjunction of the planet with Mars, its square to Saturn, and the 15° elongation from Neptune, as well as from the rising Uranus in Libra. The Sun in Taurus was more happily placed, but the close semisextile to Neptune, a contact of simulation, is of dubious moral import and was certainly employed by Hitler very frequently to further his ambitions.

As typical examples of harmonious, easy and fortunate self-expression under Venus we may refer to the two Dare sisters, who did much to inaugurate the cult of the " flapper " in the earlier part of the century. Both had Venus rising, in the one case in exaltation, in the other in Libra.

It will be apparent that in any study of self-expression, from the astrological angle, Venus has great importance. Other values do indeed express themselves readily enough, but none so freely and graciously. We will not anticipate what is to be said when considering the other planets, except to point out that Mars is the polar opposite of Venus, ruling the signs that are opposed to hers. Hence any study of the one, in theory or in practical horoscopy, calls for equal and concurrent attention to the other. And we see at once that whilst Mars is insistent upon self-expression, it commonly does so in disregard of others, whereas the self-expression of Venus goes hand-in-hand with that of others and operates through them.

Herein lies the weakness of Venus. For it is evident that conditions will and must arise when " others " will not collaborate. Either those who would are absent, or there is actual hostility. Then Venus, in herself, is powerless. We do not mean that a very Venerean person will necessarily illustrate this, for there is no horoscope that is " all Venus," but in these conditions Venus herself, as a horoscopic factor, cannot help. She will do her utmost to find absent helpers and conciliate those who are inimical to her projects ; but to work single-handed is beyond her.

Hence it arises that, in order to win helpmates, she will often become an appeaser and compromise her principles, or evince other signs of moral weakness. This does not imply that she is a physical coward, though physical sensitiveness is often considerable ; but there is a great and sometimes crippling dislike of taking a firm stand, of saying no, or of otherwise causing friction and unpleasantness.

Repeatedly we see in astrology that planets are neither benefic nor malefic ; it is a question of their being good in their own fields but useless or troublesome in others. This fact can be applied deliberately in everyday life, and each planetary value can be cultivated so that it is ready to be used when the appropriate circumstances confront us.

As well as the moral weakness that is sometimes

apparent in the Venus temperament, there is a corresponding intellectual condition which arises from the readiness of the Venus native to see and appreciate the different sides to a question. This trait, admirable in itself, sometimes inhibits action altogether, whereas it should operate as a preliminary to a right choice as to the course to be pursued. For example, in politics Venus is rarely a partisan or extremist, but it is well to take care lest this openmindedness should degenerate into mere indifference and *laissez-faire*. Venus is not overblessed with physical energy and this failing combines with the dislike of friction to cause Venus to drop out of the struggle easily and make terms at any price with its opponents.

MARS

Mars, the so-called lesser malefic, is perhaps the easiest of the planets to understand astrologically. There may be some symbolical significance in the generally accepted belief that conditions upon it more closely resemble those upon the earth than those upon any other planet of our system, so that it has been thought that life, and possibly intelligent beings, may dwell there.

As we have said, its significance in astrology is the opposite of that of Venus, and as Venus flanks the earth on the near side to the Sun, so Mars' orbit lies next beyond the terrestrial.

Venus is an essential humane planet ; Mars is said to rule the animal kingdom and the passions and appetites in man. Venus rules a sign of earth and a sign of air ; Mars rules Aries—fire, and Scorpio—water. It is possible that the more mysterious side of Scorpio is to be related rather to Pluto.

Mars is individualistic and non-co-operative. It is self-assertive ; and though not necessarily selfish in the sense of being niggardly or mean, it is little interested in the affairs of others, just as Venus has an instinct for putting itself in others' shoes. Its reactions are personal, without reference to abstract principles. It does not shirk unpleasant or dangerous work and the more objective this is, the more it lies right to hand, the better it likes it.

Personally it is brave to rash, but there is, through Scorpio, a possibility of spiritual terrors. Shakespeare's " Macbeth " is a study in the Scorpionic temperament, both in the person of the monarch himself and of his spouse. But, as we have observed, it might be truer to relegate their self-generated tormenting fears to Pluto. Still, it is well not to forget the negative aspect of Mars.

Sexual life is often placed under this planet, partly because of his general affinity with our animal nature and partly because of the rulership over Scorpio, which in turn relates to the generative organs. Probably this is partly correct. It will not infrequently be found that the signs occupied by the Sun and Mars in the map of one marriage partner are occupied by the same bodies, sometimes transposed, in that of the other. Or it may be that only one of these bodies is thus placed, e.g., Eva Braun had Mars in Taurus, the sign containing Hitler's Sun and Mars (and Venus). Venus enters into the field because man is bisexual and the sexual act requires the collaborative action that Venus rules. Marriage as a union of two separate individuals in partnership is ruled by Venus. Sexual activity in its pleasurable and also its progenitive aspect comes under the Sun. Possibly the sexual act *per se*, apart from biological or social accompaniments, is Martian. It is probable that masculine impotence is usually a correlate of a defective Mars. Frigidity in females should rather, it is thought, be related to Soli-Saturnian affliction.

Though essentially a non-mental planet, Mars in common signs or cadent houses has a strong effect upon the mind, and this is very true of its sextile aspects. Especially in the negative mutables it inclines to studies of an abstruse and arcane kind, whereas in positives it turns the mind to more open and usual pursuits, making it aggressive, disputative and dogmatic, quick and incisive.

Traditionally Mars is the planet of war, but, as with sex, this problem is not quite so simply disposed of. If marriage is the supreme symbol of union, so war pre-eminently represents separation. The one is the Conjunction, the other the Opposition.

In studying the so-called mundane maps of the recent war it was noticeable that Pluto was most often indicative of attack and aggression, as for example the conjunction of the progressed Moon with that planet in the natus of Hirohito exactly at the time of Pearl Harbour. On the other hand Venus appeared the usual significator of victory—Notre Dame de la Victoire. Thus it was exactly rising at London in the figure of the Jupiter-Saturn conjunction of August, 1940, just before the Battle of Britain, and it was also exactly on the midheaven at Tokio in the winter ingress of 1941, heralding the sweeping successes of the Japanese aggressors. Except that victories naturally bring rejoicing to the victors it is not easy to interpret this fact in terms of principles. One would have expected, if guided by traditional conceptions, that a culminating Venus would have pointed to conciliation on the part of the Japanese rather than treacherous behaviour and colossal gains, unless we regard Venus in such cases as operating through Taurus, the sign of worldly profit, or as indicating, in the case of the Battle of Britain, safety and the preservation of the country from invasion and ruin. It would not be surprising if Venus showed victory followed by peace, but in neither case was this so.

Mars seemed altogether less prominent and important in these maps than one might have expected.

This may be explained thus. Mars is a disputative, and, under distortion, a quarrelsome planet.   But modern wars are seldom of this character. In medieval times they may often have arisen as the result of personal feuds and enmities between magnates, but nowadays they are more often planned by the assailant in a quite un-Martian spirit ; they are coldly and deliberately undertaken as expressions of the will to power pure and simple, or of power as embodied in possessions.

Now the will to power is no simple phenomenon, or, if it is essentially so, it is commonly complicated in its manifestations by the intricacies of human nature. There is a will to power that is linked with sadism, the sort of power that a torturer or jailer exercises over the actual persons of his victims. There is a will to a power which is at bottom neither cruel nor benevolent, but delights in the sense of its own strength. There is a will to power to arrange and ordinate which is Saturnian.

But it may be suggested that, in any consideration of the question, Taurus, the negative sign of Venus, should be given much attention. The second house does not only denote one's financial strength ; it has a relation to one's moral and physical resources and stamina. Taurus is a great exerciser of power ; it is acknowledged to be the sign of the policeman and your Taurean parent rules his household kindly perhaps but certainly firmly.

It is noteworthy that both Hitler and Hirohito, the prime aggressors of our time, had Venus in Taurus (both, too, in aspect to Saturn).

Here then is perhaps one reason why Venus enters so largely into our modern war-maps. Perhaps it always did, but our forerunners were blinded by mythological tradition.

Again, it takes two to make a quarrel and the simplest form of warfare—the duel—is obviously a matter of personal relationships and to that extent Venusian. It is so common to find military commanders with the Sun in Libra that it is strange that few astrologers have noticed the fact.

Mars, it is suggested, wishes to have and go its own way. It fights only when others attempt to check or baffle its effort to express itself, but it does not seek battles. It is not interested in other people and would prefer to ignore them. Psychologically it is simple to the extent of *naïveté*. One is reminded of Cellini's prayer, in which he gently chid the Almighty for throwing vexatious people in his path so that he was *obliged* to kill or wound them. To the Martian it is always the other man who gets in the way. His failing does not lie in his seeking a fight, but in his inability, when thwarted, to deal with the situation in any other way than by violence.

Similarly his alleged brutality and cruelty are due to his incapacity to enter into others' feelings, his impatience, and ready resort to force as the only instrument that he understands.

He is, of course, egocentric and to that extent selfish, but in general his faults have been grossly exaggerated, especially by the old writers. He has been allowed to do much of life's hard and dangerous work and then has been maligned for his crudity and lack of refinement, just as Florence Nightingale was reviled as unladylike because she faced the horrors of military hospitals.

But in any study of self-expression this powerful and vigorous planet must be accorded the fullest attention. We may add that modern conditions have by no means reduced the number of the channels through which an ordinate and useful expression of his value can be manifested. Engineering in all its forms is to a greater or less extent under Mars, and for others there is chemistry, especially the analytical branches, surgery and scientific sanitation.

CHAPTER II

THE MAJOR PLANETS

JUPITER

THIS planet may be contrasted on the one hand with Saturn, and on the other with Mercury.

As Jupiter rules the future and movement towards progressive change, so Saturn rules the past and the preservation of the past ; as Jupiter is free, so Saturn is bound ; as Jupiter represents expansion, so Saturn stands for limitation and so on, in a series of opposites well known to astrological students.

Jupiter is pre-eminently the planet of self-expression, being in this respect, so to speak, the first agent of the Sun. Plainly there can be no self-expression without freedom ; and a life that is strictly bound by the past is to that extent incapable of expressing *itself* at all ; it can but produce repeated expressions of bygone things.

Jupiter manifests on a far broader canvass than Mercury, the ruler of the two signs that are opposed to his and which compose, with them, the mutable, common or mental cross. The vision of Gemini is normal, that of Virgo microscopic ; but Jupiter is telescopic, scanning distant horizons. Mercury studies local maps ; he is usually an authority on tubes and bus routes. But Jupiter asks for atlases and maps of continents.

Exactly the same qualities appear in the intellectual life. Jupiter seeks general principles and universal ideas, whilst Mercury is a critic and commentator, an annotator of margins.

He seems in one sense to stand between Venus, than whom he is much more energetic, and Mars, who is more drastic and crude than Jupiter, though the latter assumes a quasi-Martian recklessness quite easily. It would seem that, in some respects at any rate, Jupiter is not so purely benefic as Venus.

The love of chance and hazard that characterises our planet is easily understood. All progress, all movement into the future, demands the taking of risks. It is a question of quitting the well-trodden ways. The pioneer must take a chance ; he does not know what lies ahead of him.

But it is natural that he should desire to know as much as he can, and hence arises the interest in prediction and prophecy that are Jovian traits, as well as the simple fact that it is largely in the future that the Jovian lives mentally : he is interested in it for its own sake. Jupiter seeks new experiences, and it is only in the future as regards time and in the unknown distances as regards space that he can find them.

Hence he lacks fidelity in friendship and marriage ; when he has exhausted the experiences of one association he must look for others, or droop in boredom. If a predominantly Jovian is faithful in such matters, it is not because of his Jovianity.

Religion, too, is placed correctly under Jupiter, or at least it lies for the most part in his province. For religious thought offers scope for the widest sweeps into the mysteries of space and time, and beyond into the Eternal and Infinite. Metaphysics and philosophy come under Jupiter, for similar reasons. Then, again, must not the planet of the future, of progress, look beyond the grave ? Unless he can do so, he sees himself confronted with final frustration ; his schemes become a derision.

Similarly Jupiter is the planet of Hope. For our hopes

lie in the future. Faith, too, is under Jupiter, for faith is opposed to the hard facts of Saturn ; faith is, in a sense, taking a chance.

Jupiter is essentially a benevolent planet ; it is not merely interested in the future out of curiosity ; it wishes to see a progressive betterment in human conditions.

Law is traditionally ascribed to Jupiter, but it is clear that in many of its aspects, and especially from the standpoint of those who are subject to law, it is coercive and restrictive. This point, like others we have discussed, is not a simple one. Justice as between two contending parties is certainly under Venus. Retribution and the punishment of the transgressor would seem to be Scorpionic and Plutonian. Order, which is maintained by law, is Saturnian. Where then does Jupiter enter into the matter ? Is it as the protector of the unfortunate and helpless, as the laws should be ? Is it because true progress must be carried out in a lawful and orderly manner ? Is the attribution not merely overstressed, but actually faulty ?

The expression of Jupiter is chiefly in the mental and emotional spheres, though it is possible that the latter, related as it is to Pisces, is in process of passing to Neptune. Your Jovian can lack sympathy ; he is impatient and soon grows weary of listening to other people's troubles, but he is never deliberately cruel, however hurtful his insouciance may be to the sensitive. Intellectual speculation and argument are his principal pursuits, especially the making of plans for the future. The urge to action is strong ; he is energetic. But he is neither patient nor painstaking and is apt to lose interest when a topic or scheme has been, to his mind, exhausted. Thus we constantly find that Jupiter, without the co-operation of his opposite Saturn, is ineffective, brilliant but undependable, here one day and gone tomorrow. One would hazard the view that no planet is less use, not to say more dangerous, when it is out of hand.

A good instance is that of Lord Byron's daughter, the Countess of Lovelace, whose nativity is given in Zadkiel's " Grammar." Here a map full of brilliant aspects is spoilt by a predominance of Fire, especially of Sagittarius. Saturn, though well affected and in Aquarius, is in the 12th house. Possessing a fine intellect, she ruined herself and wasted her life pursuing the illusion of an " infallible " system for backing horses. It is not recorded whether she sought to use astrology to that end !

Jupiter rules horses and motor-cars ; the former needs the rein, and to drive a car without brakes is an operation fraught with danger to driver and public alike.

It has to be admitted, by those who have seriously studied the requisite number of cases, that Jupiter can very definitely incline to crime, and this, too, when in technical " good " aspect. The motive is probably the need to repair the ravages of extravagance or the desire to procure the means for prodigal enjoyment, luxury or splendid living. Landru had the Moon and Jupiter in conjunction ; Hopf, who poisoned several persons for insurance money (see *Modern Astrology*, August, 1915) had these bodies in trine ; as also Trenkler who killed three people in robbing a jeweller's shop (same reference) ; they were in conjunction in N.N. 271 (poisoned relatives for insurance money) ; these cases all show severe afflictions elsewhere, but the part played by Jupiter in producing the motive, if not the carrying thereof into effect, cannot be gainsaid. It is not cold and heartless, like a bad Saturn, but it can be reckless and unimaginative.

Finally, it is regarded as the planet of good fortune, and not without some reason. An angular Jupiter does, to a large extent, serve to ward off the " slings and arrows of outrageous fortune." But this aspect of the planet is not one that the children of Jupiter should hear too much about, for it may add to their innate tendency to take risks and to rely upon their luck rather than upon hard work and common-sense.

SATURN

Saturn, when operative restrictively, is the prime obstacle to free expression ; indeed, one may say that it is always hostile to *free* expression. It has its own fields and modes of expression ; and within these, and on the terms it dictates, it permits expression, but not otherwise.

We say it is the *prime* obstacle to free expression, for there are others, and important ones. These are those that arise in connection with the Water Triplicity, of which more in due course. They are quite different ; they arise from fear and the sense of inadequacy, which are not under Saturn, though Saturn often works hand-in-hand with them, and produces most difficult complexes in so doing.

Saturn may be regarded as the planet of the principle of Matter, or at any rate as the planet that has most affinity with matter, if we regard this as " a barrier, a vast obstructive bulk of chaos and deadness, interposing between life and some non-material goal that lies beyond " (*Guide to Modern Thought*, by C. E. M. Joad, Chap. VI, on Vitalism and Creative Evolution). But this is by no means the whole significance of Saturn, nor indeed can the notion of chaos be considered appropriate to the planet ; its obstructive quality is founded upon rigid order, not upon confusion, which is a Neptune-Pisces condition.

Nor need we regard this obstructive function as necessarily evil, as in fact Joad, in the chapter cited above, clearly perceives. It can have a stimulative effect upon the force that feels itself obstructed. Furthermore, without the limitations of form, existence in the objective world, and thought in the subjective, would be impossible. For effective thought must be founded upon clearly defined ideas.

The obstruction of Saturn is sometimes derived from the self, as for instance in personal indolence or stupidity. It is also very frequently the result of actions for which the subject is in no way responsible and over which he has little or no control. These actions are often those of older people (e.g., the parents) or of those who are in authority over him, as the government. For example, some new law or other change in the social organism may interfere adversely with his business or other enterprises.

He represents the ultimate expression of the thoughts of God in the mundane spheres of precipitated existence, because these are the most definite and limited of all things. Hence he is pre-eminently the *practical* planet.

He has, indeed, a value anterior to the mundane world, for through Aquarius he is a thinker and planner, profound, careful and exact. But it is rarely that a Saturn-value in the horoscope has not a direct external expression in our lives. The Sun, for instance, when configured with Saturn affects our worldly career almost inevitably, often beginning with the affairs of the father in their effects upon the native himself. Sun opposed to Saturn in the map of Kaiser William II shows the tragic lot of the father and the lack of sympathy between him and the native. It shows the basic weakness of character of the Kaiser himself, his temporary successes and his ultimate downfall. In a sense he was not (at least in terms of the present life) to be blamed ; it was destiny and could not have been otherwise, at least in broad outline. Few people can be wholly blamed for what befalls them under a configuration such as this ; circumstances are too much for them. The Czar Nicholas II had ruler and Sun opposed to Saturn ;

his son, the Czarevitch, had Sun opposed to Saturn. In none of these cases was the native a bad man; but they were weak, or too weak for their circumstances. In the case of the Czarevitch he was, of course, a helpless child.

Such things seem a denial of justice. But observe that Saturn harks back into the past, and this is equally true whether we judge the matter from a materialistic point of view and mean inherited conditions both physical and circumstantial, as when a monarch inherits a perilous throne, or whether we accept the adage " as ye sow so shall ye reap " with a reference to the sins and errors of previous existences.

Saturn is the symbol of strict retributive justice. Perhaps that is shown in his affinity with Libra, though this may also indicate the need that justice should be tempered with mercy.

In those countries that come under this planet the social organism tends strongly to reflect the principle of order, often carried to excess, as in the modern caste-system of India, which represents the over-development of an older and simpler system. In other Capricorn countries, as for instance in ancient Mexico, religion demanded huge blood-sacrifices. Some Aquarian states, as Prussia and Czarist Russia, repressed the lower classes long after these had attained comparative freedom in other countries. Saturn may be obsessed with the ideal of law and order to the exclusion of the complementary ideals of Venus and Jupiter, not to mention those of Uranus. It does not only pursue its own expression but tries to repress that of other planetary values.

In varying degrees all those in authority should study the true expression of Saturn and scrutinise their own behaviour in the exercise of power in that light.

In considering the question of vocation we pay regard to inner aptitudes, likes and dislikes, parents' wishes, and what is financially and physically possible. All four points may be affected by Saturn, but especially the last two. Thus, Saturn in the 10th house squaring a strong rising planet will tend to indicate a sharp conflict between the personal wishes as regards a profession and what is possible or what is enforced.

In every horoscope in which the Moon and Saturn are strong the influence of the family will fall heavily on the native and will largely influence his unfoldment. The former will operate principally in psychological ways, but Saturn will affect chiefly the external expression, and there-after react upon the psyche. Its action is from without inwards ; it is the embodiment of the not-self. Thus it may produce the truly " worldly " man. That is, the world will enter into the ego and build itself into its being.

This worldly aspect of the planet has led some writers to commit the etymological atrocity of saying that Saturn is Satan.

But a good Saturn, or a good response to Saturn if we wish to speak less deterministically, is one of the best features that a map can display. So long as conscientious work, prudence, punctuality, common-sense, and tem-perate and well-controlled habits have any worth, so long will Saturn, rightly understood and interpreted in our lives, be a planet of the utmost value. It is when we wish to dictate to him and extort by violence or cunning what *we* think will be good for us that he becomes, in our eyes, a tyrant.

Attempts to " drive " Saturn are usually a waste of time and energy ; if he can be in any sense overcome it is by patience and industrious persistence.

Saturn has little operation in the sphere of the emotions; he merely chills and represses them, for our moods are by nature lawless, vague and formless and insusceptible of order. Saturn, however, is a faithful planet and he introduces fidelity into our affectional life, even if the affections are usually concentrated upon few objects. He is the planet of friendship, through affinity with Aquarius, but that is not to say that he has, as is said, " a large circle of friends " ; rather he may know many people and have two or three to whom he will be a true and abiding friend.

In the mental sphere he operates to give care and precision, and he *can* be so slow in reaching his conclusions that he appears stupid, and perhaps is so from a Mercurial standpoint. But what he lacks in mental flexibility and quick perception, he gains in judgment and common-sense ; it is worth waiting a little for his pronouncements, for when they come they usually merit consideration. But in those vocations that call for quick decision, e.g., naval and military commands, he fails through slowness, and it is probable that an over-Saturnian commander would be always on the defensive.

It is often said that an afflicted Saturn, especially in the midheaven, foreshadows final downfall. But it generally raises the native first, for the reason perhaps that one cannot fall unless one has first of all risen. Such a position often tempts the native, through ambition, to try things beyond his strength ; but a helpful Saturn will have a contrary effect, for he will give the ability to gauge possibilities judiciously. The classic case of Saturn in the midheaven having this significance was Napoleon, whose data, however, are uncertain. Hitler's are better founded and in his case it must be noted how very badly placed his Saturn was. Any planet in the 10th house, equally afflicted, would have shown grave dangers, though probably less dramatic ones.

We shall discuss the relation of Saturn to Aquarius elsewhere, except to say at this point that it is chiefly on this side of its operation that Saturn affects our morality, using that word in the somewhat negative and restricted sense often associated with Victorianism.   As ruler of Aquarius Saturn is a social planet, but intellectually so, not emotionally.   It is concerned in the right ordering of society, and here its relation to our moral life, in the sense of conformity to established and respected customs and manners, appears.   And here, as we have said, its action is rather in the way of telling what not to do than in stimulating us to right moral conduct.   Its code is rigid and its penalties are strictly enforced.   Against these the more vital planets are apt to rebel.

Students of the Freudian school of thought will perceive that Saturn, in his aspect as the guardian of our personal standards of propriety, is the Censor, who is regarded as a sort of moral policeman, charged with the function of preventing any disreputable elements in the unconscious, of the existence of which the conscious mind would prefer to remain in ignorance, from forcing their way into the consciousness.   In this function Saturn becomes the antagonist of Pluto, a planet which symbolises all such eruptive action.

We now pass beyond the planetary scheme as it was known to the ancients.

It has been often observed, with regard to the three planets discovered in modern times, that the world-conditions at the time of discovery have often thrown much light upon their astrological significance. Uranus was first detected, by William Herschel, in 1781.   It was then in Gemini.   This was the year which was to see the surrender of Cornwallis to the Franco-American armies in America, an event which virtually ended the War of Independence.   The French Revolution was near at hand.

Revolution was in the air. There were the Industrial and the Romantic revolutions. . . .

There were physical peculiarities to note in the new planet. Its axis has an extreme inclination to the plane of the ecliptic (82°) and its moons rotate in a contrary sense to that of the planets.

Its nature, in broad outline, seems soon to have been settled. It was not interpreted kindly. It was said to cause stubbornness, self-will, eccentricity, with a touch of genius. The conception thus early formed has persisted.

However, not all persons born with a rising Uranus are very noticeably erratic nor are they by any means all gifted with genius. Perhaps few of them would be called " ordinary " people ; but those who conform most nearly to the usual types of mankind may be described as forthright, outspoken, subject to outbursts of anger of a rather violent kind, and frequently interested in unusual matters, though they are by no means invariably the cranks that some have considered them. They do not necessarily lack kindness, usually of an impulsive kind. There is generally dark hair, dark eyes and a swarthy complexion.

No decision has ever been reached as to the sign ruled by Uranus, if any. Here American students seem to have gone further than British in transferring Aquarius to the new planet ; but it is not known whether much real evidence has ever been adduced to support this. Certainly the physical appearance, as briefly sketched above, is very unlike the Aquarian ; it is much more reminiscent of some Martian types.* There are several ways in which such a problem can be attacked. For example, by noting

*The author has known two persons with Mars rising in Gemini who not only closely resembled each other, but also closely conformed to his conception of the Uranus type.

the sign usually rising in the map of the partner of those in whose nativities Uranus is the marriage significator.

Psychologically Aquarians seem more detached than the Uranian, who is often intellectual and scientific but seems to have a livelier emotional nature than the Aquarian.

When afflicted by such planets as Mars or Jupiter we may find Uranus very violent and revolutionary in his actions, and extremely self-willed. There is something electric about him. Undoubtedly Uranian manifestation is not generally easy.

When he is well placed he makes a good administrator or governor and it is certain that this planet favours official positions rather than trade.

He is, in fact, much influenced by the urge for power, and as between obeying and exercising authority, he will always seek the latter, even though, if the planet is badly afflicted, he will probably be a would-be tyrant, or at most very uncertain in his behaviour. Probably the inner demand for power is due to a yet deeper quality : the hatred of being controlled, the love of individual freedom. Most Uranians would probably prefer (like many Martians) to be allowed to go their own ways and live their own lives ; but, if it is necessary to occupy some recognised place in the social organism, then an authoritative one is chosen and responsibility is not shirked.

We would say that Uranus, if not exactly, as is sometimes said, " the planet of the Will," is certainly very wilful, and there is a strong manifestation on that side. Likewise he is intellectual but seldom loses " the common touch "—to use the phrase of a writer who had the planet rising at birth. Nor is he weak on the emotional level, but indulges in intense dislikes, being sensitive to slights and possibly vindictive. Thus there is potentially a very complete development, usually with a special self-expression along a particular line, often an un-common one.

The best word, perhaps, to describe the typical afflicted-Uranus person is that of *perversity ;* he tends to take hold of every stick by the wrong end. He is his own worst enemy and often throws away the results of his labours by some inexplicable act of folly. Indeed, one difficult aspect to Uranus will often appear to be responsible for ruining an otherwise excellent geniture.

Uranus has a bad name in all matters of the sexes. Here his heterodox views and erratic conduct are calculated to upset a partner whose own ideas are of a more conven-tional pattern ; but it is probable that the less exacting standards of our own days render it easier for him to bear the yoke of matrimony.

It seems, then, that for the more normal Uranian—that is, for the man or woman who has the planet prominent but not ill-affected—there are two main channels of self-expression in the active world : officialdom and science, or, if Venus and Neptune are strong, art. There is a distinct connection between the planet and government, whether local or national. If Uranus is helpful, the help often comes through these channels, or perhaps from powerful and highly-reputable institutions, such as universities. On the other hand, the native who bears the burden of an ill-placed Uranus usually falls foul of such things. Shelley, who was sent down from Oxford, is a case in point, even if one may say that his Uranus was powerful rather than dangerous except for the special times and circumstances in which he lived.

If Uranus is prominent but badly afflicted, advice becomes difficult, nor will the native be likely to listen to good counsel. It is probable that he will drift into unortho-dox and perhaps revolutionary company and be a failure from the standpoint of the conventional.

Lack of patience is a common failing and there are often nervous difficulties and inhibitions.

We find, therefore, that Uranus is commonly one of the most interesting and at the same time difficult planets so far as self-expression goes. It usually possesses some abilities but they are not easily directed into right channels unless the planet itself is well placed and the figure of birth otherwise well poised. It is the planet that has, figuratively, broken out of the ring of the Saturnian orbit with its accumulated wisdom. Tradition, which is the experience of the race, means little to it. Its interests tend to the ultra-modern or the definitely old ; it dislikes the average and is the born nonconformist. In this sense it is opposed to Saturn in significance and agrees better with Jupiter, except that, in place of the more natural growth signified by that planet, it likes to progress by leaps and plunges.

It seems to express itself best through constructive contacts with Mercury, Jupiter and the Sun ; it is less happy with the Moon or Venus. In difficult aspects to Mars and Saturn it becomes definitely fraught with danger. The same is the case when it afflicts weak planets in weak signs (e.g., Moon or Venus in Pisces) for then its perversive propensity is very likely to produce serious results, as for example in N.N. 271 (poisoned grandmother, husband and brother for insurance money), Moon conjunction Jupiter in Pisces, normally a most gentle formation, is perverted by the opposition of Uranus.

NEPTUNE

This planet was discovered in 1846, being then retrograde in 25½ Aquarius. Its single satellite, like those of Uranus, has a retrograde motion.

The conditions of the times when it was discovered reveal, once again, political unrest with a certain revival of nationalism, over against socialist developments. British colonial slaves were emancipated in 1833. Robert Owen began his propaganda in 1834 and the Chartist movement started in 1836. The Corn Laws were repealed in 1846. The year 1848 is especially associated with revolutions in Europe.

It seems plain that the discovery of each new planet has ushered in fresh conditions tantamount to revolution, and if others are found in the future, the same will doubtless be the case. It remains to differentiate their motives and methods, if we can. The American and French revolutions, which were Uranian, were accompanied by much bloodshed ; those of Neptune were not, at least to the same extent.

Neptune is commonly regarded as concerned rather with philanthropy, art and certain cryptic studies and pursuits such as spiritualism, than with politics ; but the events around 1846 seem to alter the picture so as to include the last of these. The modern spiritist movement is said to have started in 1848, when the Fox sisters began their demonstrations.*

It may be conceded without much danger that Neptune has a connection with various forms of crypticism, including astrology.

Secondly, that it is related to the arts and especially to music and painting, and the drama.

Thirdly, that it has an affinity with love for the helpless and exploited and perhaps most of all for animals.

Fourthly, that there is a relation to the sea and marine matters.

There can be little question as to Neptune having a

*It is said that they began to bring their tricks before the public under the influence of a married sister named Fish !

strong kinship with Pisces. This seems much plainer than the alleged link between Uranus and Aquarius.

But it is a certain Protean changefulness and elusiveness about the planet that have made him the most difficult of all astrological factors to elucidate fully. The radical idea seems to escape determination. The Neptunian, and Neptunian conditions, are always other than they seem. Hence the ability of those with the planet strong to act well, both legitimately upon the stage and criminally in such things as the confidence-trick. Yet many Neptunians have a strong sense of honour and are personally frank and even direct.

Well placed, Neptune often shows uncommon good fortunes, but these are sometimes more on paper than substantial. As an afflictor the planet is in some respects more difficult than Saturn.

From an inner point of view he is the significator of various forms of hypersensitiveness. He is fastidious. He can inflict severe self-consciousness, shyness and stage-fright. He is self-distrustful and the physique is rarely robust, though not necessarily sickly. Irrational fears are often generated under planetary configurations in which the planet plays a prominent part. The commonest psychological trait is worry, again an expression of self-distrust.

Neptune does not check our self-expression in the decisive manner associated with Saturn ; he perplexes, baffles and wears down with anxieties. As the retiarius in the arena of the Romans threw his bewildering and impeding net round the muscular scutarius, so Neptune casts a net of intricacies and uncertainties round his victim. He is the will-o'-the-wisp and the mountain mist. That son of Neptune, Peer Gynt, meets him in the Boyg.

Thus it is necessary for those in whose maps he appears

as an afflictive factor to eschew everything that is not well known and well tried, sedulously to distrust appearances, and to avoid as far as possible all complex and intricate conditions.

His ordinate expression will undoubtedly be, in most cases, in the field of the arts. He has also a distinct affinity with chemical studies. There are also possibilities in the way of nursing, detective work, and social and animal welfare. For the less developed intellectually, there is the sea and the liquor trade.

There seem points in common with Sagittarius, as well as Pisces, and it is possible that Neptune is a planet of religion, but, as we have said, he appears to tend to spiritualistic phenomenalism more often than to intellectual and philosophical studies.

In sum, we would not say that Neptune itself is a planet that finds difficulty in self-expression ; it is in its influence upon other planets, when in contact with them, that it creates trouble. It tends to create illusions and destroy the sense of reality. It blurs the clarity of one's perceptions, throwing a haze over the actual. It has a kinship with the so-called " unconscious " and creates fantasies of the origin of which the dreamer is ignorant.

It can be visionary and idealistic beyond any other planet, but only a study of the whole nativity can determine whether the visions are likely to be rational or mere fanciful imaginings.

The self-expressive activities of Neptune must, then, of necessity be beset by certain dangers, yet none can deny that they include some of the highest reaches of human achievement.

Amongst the other planets it would seem that it has least affinity with Mars and Saturn, both objective in their values. It agrees best with the Moon and Jupiter and can indicate very beautiful expression through contact with Mercury, which also has an elusive quality, and with Venus.

PLUTO

Though discovered as recently as 1930 (in 17° Cancer) the basic significance of this body is not difficult to determine.

It is the resurrection or resurgence of the past—the forgotten or half-forgotten past—in the present. Not for nothing is this period associated with the great vogue of Freudian psycho-analysis and also with the rise of the Nazi doctrines, which in the end produced an eruption of brutality which the world at large had never dreamt of beholding again. In this sense Pluto is the skeleton in the cupboard and the slumbering volcano.

The planet is small in size and very distant and some have denied its statue as a true planet, asserting that they can find no evidence of its action in the natal horoscope. Its orbit lies at an angle of some $17\frac{1}{2}°$ to the ecliptic, with the result that the zodiacal degree to which it is referred may be on the ascendant when the body of the planet is at a considerable distance from it, and so also with other house positions. This may complicate investigation.

Howbeit, it appears to have a definite value in mundane maps, as we mentioned when discussing the subject of War on page 26. Its exact parallel with Hitler's ascendant may or may not be fortuitous. To us it seems a pagan, indeed a feral, influence, in its lower manifestations.

We have little hesitation in associating it with Scorpio and have found its directions indicative of death and disease on the one hand and of improved health on the other.

But perhaps a more fundamental significance of this

planet is that which I have ventured to associate with the
ancient Latin deity Janus, of whom it is said (Smith's
Classical Dictionary) that he is " the god of all beginnings
both in public and private life, of the birth of man and of
the opening of the year." Further, " Janus was the god
of the doorway (ianua) who guarded all that went out and
came in." He was not, however, god of beginnings only,
but also of closings, having the appellations Patulcius
(from *pătere*, to lie open) and Clusius (from *claudĕre*, to
close).

It has been observed that Plutonic directions often
indicate either the beginning of a chapter in the life or the
closing of one. Its action, unlike that of Uranus, is not
necessarily violent or unexpected. The point is that it
does not produce a fresh development of existing movements, but an altogether new departure. Other types of
directions (notably those of Jupiter) may have a similar
value ; but this characteristic seems peculiarly Plutonic.

Death itself is, of course, the closing of a chapter in a
special but very true sense.

So, too, is birth the opening of a chapter. And it is
worth noting that Janus, or Ianus, is considered to be a
masculine form of Diana, the initial " D " having been
lost in the male form. Diana, under the title of Lucina
(" she who brings to the light of day "), was associated
with parturition.

This aspect of Pluto might perhaps be denominated as
" Pluto-Janus."

Pluto as the bringer to light of that which has lain
buried in the collective or individual subconscious,
the " raiser of the dead," might possibly be called
" Pluto-Titan." It will be recalled how the Titans
attempted to storm Olympus and seize power from the
Olympians gods, but were hurled down into Tartarus,
where they lay struggling " pent in regions of laborious

breath." In particular Enceladus was said to lie pinned under Mount Aetna and to shake Sicily with his heavings.

The Titans belong to early Pelasgian cults which were driven underground when the Achaean tribes invaded Greece from the north, bringing with them the worship of the Homeric gods, and they were later taken as symbols of the wild and barbaric elements in human nature which struggle against the rational and spiritual principles of light.

However, it can hardly be supposed that the name Pluto (however we may modify it with secondary epithets) has no basis in fact. It would seem that, so close and real is the relation between man and the planetary bodies, appropriate titles have invariably been chosen for the latter, even though those who gave them would have ridiculed the suggestion that in doing so they were " guided " or " inspired."

Probably, therefore, the normal expression of Plutonic values would largely coincide with those ascribed to Mars, and, in particular, to Mars-Scorpio, i.e., those of the analyser, inspector, and investigator. Nevertheless the author cannot claim, up to the present, to have verified this from observed data. It must, therefore, be presented purely as an hypothesis.

CHAPTER III

ASPECTS AND EXALTATIONS

IT is the view of the author that all multiples of 15°
produce valid aspects, even though a narrow orb must be
applied to such distances as 15°, 75° and 105°. In his
personal experiences important results have coincided
with the formation, by the progressed Sun, of aspects of
these denominations. Indeed, he would rate them as
more potent than the Quintile series.

It seems reasonable, too, to expect the division of the
circle by 7 and 9 to yield valid contacts, i.e., of 51° 26′ and
40°, with their principal derivatives.

As to which of these aspects would be classed as " good "
and which as " bad " only experience can show.

Indeed, the principal problem arising from the subject
is to decide what we mean by " good " and " bad " aspects
and how far and in what sense these distinctions are true
to nature.

When the author was engaged upon compiling lists of
persons with similar aspects, in the course of preparing his
book on this matter,* he arranged the lists according as
the contacts were technically benefic or malefic. But often
it was borne upon him that it was extremely difficult to see
in what way the fortunes and careers of the persons whose
aspects appeared in the one class differed from those
placed in the other.

To take a case in point. Cecil Rhodes had Sun trine
Neptune ; F. D. Roosevelt had them in square. Yet the
two cases have strong points of resemblance. Both men
were crippled by grievous disease, each achieved great

*The Astrological Aspects, published by L. N. Fowler & Co., Ltd.

political success, each was regarded, by his opponents, as unscrupulous, one attained and the other inherited great wealth.

As a result, the writer is inclined to lay great stress on the essential character of the planet concerned in any formation especially in regard to the particular matter being considered, according as this may or may not be congenial to the planet's nature ; and also upon its strength by sign and house.   In a word no cut-and-dried descriptions and classifications will do ; the matter is not so simple as that, as the young student will gradually find out for himself.

In any case, " good " and " bad " are ambiguous words. Sometimes we use them in a moral sense ; sometimes we mean by them only what we happen to like or dislike, as when we speak of good or bad food or weather.

Some use the words *constructive* and *destructive*, but these, though often appropriate, are by no means always so.

One of the things most noticeable about the good aspects is that they are *conformative ;* they tend to make the subject swim with the tide, or, like Mr. Pickwick, to shout with the larger crowd.   On the other hand the " bad " ones make the native out of tune with his surroundings— shall we say *incompliant ?* —which may enhance his moral reputation but not his comfort.

Then, the opposition and square are usually stronger than the trine and sextile and so lead to extremes.   From this point of view *temperate* and *excessive* seem appropriate terms.

Again, trines and sextiles may be called *facilitative* inasmuch as they tend to help our endeavours, and squares and oppositions are *tensive* or (in fixed signs or when Saturn is involved) *obstructive*. The semisquare and sesquiquadrate are *frictional* and the quincunx is often *solvent*, bringing difficulties to the point whereat they begin to dissolve.

It is of interest to observe that Aristippus, a contemporary of Socrates, taught (according to Smith's *Dictionary*) that " sensation consisted in motion, and he distinguished two kinds of motion, the rough producing pain and the smooth producing pleasure, the absence of motion being a neutral state." There seems a definite likeness here to the astrological doctrine of the good, bad and neutral aspects.

It may be said that this matter of terminology is not very important and that it is convenient (as indeed it is) to speak of good and bad planets and aspects.

But convenience is not the only consideration involved.

There is the fact, which we have tried to stress, that it is very doubtful whether aspects *can* be rightly classed in the definitive manner that the use of these terms implies. In any case, their use tends to take the student's attention away from the general strength of the planets concerned and to concentrate it entirely upon the matter of aspects, which often leads to wrong conclusions.

Further, the employment of these words " good " and " bad " has a quite deplorable effect upon astrologers themselves and upon the lay public that listens to them. It gives the impression of a childish and ignoble attitude of mind towards life and tends to make us actually adopt such a standpoint.

True, those who consult astrologers when in trouble should be prepared to hear the truth, but there are ways and ways of presenting this sometimes disagreeable commodity to persons who are probably already worried and depressed.

To tell a consultant that he is faced with a " bad aspect " is likely to impress him with the notion that he is confronted with something that has neither rime nor reason, but is simply unpleasant, vexatious and perhaps dangerous. To tell him that an approaching aspect is difficult should have a quite different effect. It implies that there will be a job to do or a problem to solve, not just brute disaster ahead. It is a challenge, not a crude threat.

In the matter of self-expression the term bad is particularly inappropriate, for many squares and oppositions tend to promote rather than hinder our development. In fact here the danger may lie in too free and vigorous action and feeling, though not, of course, if Saturn is repressively involved. There is a possibility that the will may be erratic and unreasonably directed. Judgments may be precipitate and reckless. Emotions may be almost uncontrollable. But there is more, not less, activity.

For example, the typical Mercury trine Jupiter person will be pious, whereas the quadrature between the same planets would rather indicate a critical attitude towards religion with tendencies either to believe too readily and lapse into superstition or to treat religious matters superficially and flippantly. But it might also, if Saturn were strong, point to a life-long search after truth in these matters, which may be more painful but is also more noble than a simple acceptance of orthodoxy.

In the writer's view this example points to the essential *raison d'être* of the so-called bad aspects and the conditions in human life that they symbolise. The Creator has made the world infinitely beautiful and interesting beyond bounds, but He has not made it comfortable ; that task has to be performed by man himself, to be earned, in fact. This seems indisputable whatever we may feel about it. Without the " bad aspects " we should merely vegetate or evolve very very slowly, as does the subhuman creation.

A good, useful and enjoyable life does not, therefore, depend upon having a number of trines and sextiles,

although a totally tensive geniture might turn to a destructive manifestation or sink under the stress denoted by
such a horoscopic condition.

What is important is an *integration* of the factors in the
map. The weakest of all maps are those in which there are
few important contacts of any kind, with uncongenial
sign-positions and poor house emplacement.

Equally important is *balance*, as was exemplified in the
case of the Countess of Lovelace cited on page 33.

Indeed, it may even be said that all evil, as it is portrayed
horoscopically, resolves itself into lack of balance, and it
is largely because the square and opposition are so very
strong that they are often productive of unfortunate results ;
they overstress some part of the nature and create a
propensity to disease, either of character, body or fortunes.
They upset the equilibrium. Even trines can do this, but
they are less apparent in their effects because they normally fall in the same element. On the other hand two
squares, if they be of opposite tendencies, can to some
extent cancel each other out.

Integration implies that a map has an ordered significance, strong and clear in its indications and without
notably weak planets.

Mussolini's nativity may be classed as strongly integrated. The Sun is in its own sign with Mercury and they
are in sextile to four bodies in Gemini, harmonising the
life-urge with the mental powers. There is a great " fan "
formation, Uranus and Neptune being in close trine, with
Venus and Jupiter between them and in sextile to both.

It is true that a cruel and crafty nature is shown by the
Moon, besieged between Mars and Saturn, and that the
semisquare of Uranus to the Sun and Mercury perverts
both mind and will. But it is a strong map and the native
rose from being a blacksmith's son to become, for a time,
the most important person in Europe.

Hitler, we think, owed much to circumstances and to the psychological weakness of his nation. His natus evinces less obvious integration. There is one powerful formation. The Sun is in semisextile to Neptune, only 3′ from

THE NATIVITY OF BENITO MUSSOLINI
ERECTED ACCORDING TO THE METHOD OF CAMPANUS

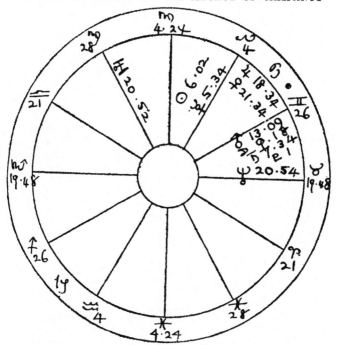

The map is drawn for 1.58 p.m., 29th July, 1883, near Milan.

exactitude, and this technically minor contact played an enormous part in his life. But the point to observe is that Mars and Venus are at the midpoint between the Sun and Neptune, about 15° from both ; and these carry with them the square of a dominant Saturn. This formation, then, involves five bodies quite closely, and to some extent Pluto also.

But Pluto is mainly concerned as being close parallel to the rising degree and in sesquiquadrate to Uranus;

THE NATIVITY OF ADOLF HITLER
ERECTED ACCORDING TO THE METHOD OF CAMPANUS

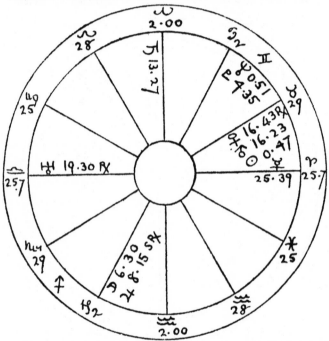

The map is erected for the recorded time, 6.30 p.m., C.E.T., 20th April, 1889, at Braunau, but it has been stated that there was difficulty in establishing respiration and so it is possible the native was born under Scorpio.

here is the restless, tensive condition with a perpetual itch towards aggression, aggravating the already acquisitive and ambitious propensities of the Taurus-afflicted-by-Saturn complex.

Moon and Jupiter stand somewhat alone, but are linked by disposal with Saturn, in whose sign they stand ; they are well configurated with the Sun.

Mercury is the weak planet. As in Mussolini's case it is in stress with Uranus, though not very closely ; again, it is in conjunction, but not closely, with the Sun. It is opposed to the ascendant. Hitler could not use clear precise thought and so he fell back upon his famous intuitions, in his case probably a sort of psychic guess-work. His natus has no signs whatever of true intuition or even sound instincts. The Water trigon is vacant ; that of Fire has nothing helpful.

However, it may be doubted whether the psychology of Hitler can be understood by reference to his natus alone. For one thing, much may be learnt from comparing his geniture with the map of the German Empire, established at Versailles on 18 January, 1871, at about one hour past noon, local time. Here, for instance, the place of Neptune falls on that of Hitler's Uranus and that of Pluto on his Venus-Mars conjunction. Other pertinent maps exhibit similar planetary coincidences.

The eminence of eminent men is not merely a matter of their own nativities. It results from the interaction thereof with other circumstantially related horoscopes, of which there may, as in such an instance as that of Hitler, be several or even many.

No man liveth unto himself alone. If astrologers neglect this great truth it is not so much through ignorance as through lack of data.

A final point is as to the relative values of applying and separating contacts.

Some have gone so far as to affirm that the latter have no value at all, which may be dismissed as an ignorant and nonsensical opinion. *Prima facie*, one may be tempted to suppose that applying aspects are stronger ; but it might also be argued that a contact that was exact just prior to birth might be stronger than one that only completes itself when the child is already born and his nativity determined.

I have no evidence that would justify me in venturing any view at all on this matter.

EXALTATIONS

As regards sign-position, and, in particular, the exaltations, it is well to recall that the ancients regarded the positive sign as showing the good, and the negative sign the evil, expressions of a planet. And this view does not seem to be altogether unfounded, for statistical investigation* has shown that Mars in Scorpio, and still more Jupiter in Pisces and Saturn in Capricorn, are distinctly accident-prone. Generally, a planet in its own sign is thought to be stronger—Saturn in Capricorn is, so to say, double-Saturn—rather than necessarily better in operation. On the other hand, a body in its exaltation is deemed to be purified and inclined to express itself well.

The scheme of exaltations handed down to us from antiquity is by no means haphazard in its arrangement, but the rationale thereof does not appear to have been noticed by modern writers and may, therefore, bear repetition, although we have set it forth elsewhere.†

The Sun, the primal vital urge or life-force, is exalted in the sign of Mars, the lesser malefic. Mars in turn is exalted in the sign of the greater malefic, Saturn. This body in turn is exalted in the sign of Venus, the lesser benefic, and Venus is exalted in the sign of the greater benefic, Jupiter, which in turn is exalted in Cancer, the sign of the Moon.

*See the author's *Astrology of Accidents*, page 20.
†See the author's *Zodiac and the Soul*, 2nd edition.

We thus obtain a circle of manifestation, starting with the positive Luminary and ending with the negative. Pluto would seem to rule the bottom of this circle, the Subterranean, Hades the Unseen, the Nether Realms. Mercury may be placed in the centre, the Messenger between kingdom and kingdom.

As for Uranus and Neptune, it may be that they rule, respectively, the Descent and the Ascent. Or perhaps Neptune should be placed at the top, opposed to Pluto, and Uranus should have a position beside Mercury, of whom he is held by many to be a higher octave.

	Neptune	
The Sun		The Moon
Mars	Mercury	Jupiter
	Uranus	
Saturn		Venus
	Pluto	

Apart from the traditional exaltations, another simple scheme suggests itself.

Exaltation means a lifting-up, and it is interesting to note that there appears to be some connection between the traditional exaltations, and the ascendant-midheaven relationship. Here, of course, latitude enters in, and the question must arise whether exaltations alter according to the place of birth.

Speaking from the standpoint of our own part of the world, we find that when the solar sign Leo rises either Aries, the Sun's traditional exaltation, or Taurus, a sign in which the Sun is admittedly strong, occupies the midheaven.

When Cancer rises, the midheaven is held by Pisces, a sign very congenial to the Moon.

When the Mercurial signs rise, we have either Aquarius

on the midheaven, which some have claimed to be the true exaltation of Mercury, or else, in the case of Virgo, the companion sign of Mercury, Gemini.

When the Venus signs rise, we get, in the case of Taurus, the sign Capricorn, never, so far as I know, regarded as in affinity with Venus. But Libra rising puts Cancer on the M.C. and this is certainly a favourable position for Venus, preferable (it might be argued) to Pisces.

When Aries rises the traditional exaltation-sign of Mars is on the midheaven; when Scorpio rises, we have Virgo, which is possibly a good sign for Mars and certainly not a bad one.

When Sagittarius rises we have Libra, traditionally the sign in which Jupiter " joys," on the M.C., and when the Fish rise, Sagittarius occupies this cusp.

When Capricorn rises we have Scorpio on the midheaven and this I regard as a sign very apt to bring out the best of Saturn, as is exemplified in the case of Goethe and Sir Humphry Davy. It may indeed be pleasanter in Libra but it does better work in Scorpio. It is true that Aquarius on the ascendant means Sagittarius on the midheaven, a sign that most might regard as a bad domicile for Saturn; but if we regard Aquarius as ruled by Uranus, then we may truly say that Sagittarius, with its love of freedom and the unconventional, has affinity with the planet.

Apart from this scheme, and the traditional one, there are certain positions of notable sign-strength. For example, Mercury is indisputably strong in Capricorn and Mars in Leo. However, here the planets are in their own trigons. This is, nevertheless, only a partial explanation, for the same thing does not always hold; Luna is not strong in Scorpio, nor Mars in Pisces, nor Venus in Virgo, despite community of element.

CHAPTER IV

THE POSITIVE-NEGATIVE POLARITY

TRADITIONALLY there are three principal divisions of the zodiac: into masculine and feminine signs, into the cardinal, fixed and common quadruplicities, and into the four triplicities.

In recent years other groupings have been suggested. There is, for example, a valuable division of the signs into three consecutive groups of four each, which W. H. Sampson* names respectively Primitive or Elemental (Aries-Taurus-Gemini-Cancer), Individual (Leo-Virgo-Libra-Scorpio) and Universal (Sagittarius-Capricorn-Aquarius-Pisces).

Again, one can contrast the first six with the last six, or, more emphatically, the first two with the last two. It can be statistically demonstrated that violent criminals tend in their genitures to planetary positions in Aries and Taurus, and to a less extent in Gemini. On the other hand, the last two are often prominent in the maps of those who tend towards idealism: they are the dreamers of dreams. Each class has its appropriate virtues and failings.

We must also note that the further we progress through the zodiac, the wider the scope of the sign-significance becomes. Thus, Gemini is the limited factual mind; Sagittarius is exploratory speculative thought. Leo is individual man *par excellence ;* Aquarius is collective man, society.

Thus even a cursory consideration of a nativity reveals much.

*The Zodiac : A Life-Epitome, W. H. Sampson.

Naturally planetary aspects affect the significance of powerful groupings ; nevertheless when these occur, and one or more sectors of the zodiac are strongly tenanted, these have a fundamental meaning. To pore over aspects and to miss these satellitia is to overlook the wood in counting the trees.

The division of the signs into positive and negative, in alternation, is of course known to every student. It repeats, in terms of the signs, the planetary division symbolised pre-eminently by the masculine Sun and the feminine Moon. It is of profound importance.

It is a commonplace in all so-called mystical teaching, and it is a fact easily confirmed by thought and observation, that the unitary principle of Being, which in its manifestation is Life, assumes immediately upon expressing itself a twofold character. This principle of polarity dominates the entire field of the Manifest.

It would be superfluous to give an exhaustive account (if this were possible) of the ways and forms in which this truth is expressed in mystical literature. So far as Christian and Hebraic thought is concerned, we find it at the very beginning in the Garden of Eden under the names of Adam and Eve, even if not earlier, in the contrast between original darkness and manifest light. Again, it appears in the Tree of the Knowledge of Good and Evil.

God and devil, good and evil, Ormuzd and Ahriman, spirit and matter, freedom and fate, energy and substance, life and death, health and sickness, action and inaction, yang and yin, Uranus and Gaia, animus and anima—these are but very few of the typical dyads.

To those who prefer later thought we may quote from Freud : " I have combined the instincts for self-preservation and for the preservation of the species under the concept of Eros and have contrasted with it an instinct of death or destruction . . . the picture which life presents to us is the result of the working of Eros and the death-instinct together and against each other " (*The Problem of Lay Analyses*, 1927, pp. 290, 291).

It is not our present intention to discuss why this twofold expression follows on the Primal Unity of Being, unless to say that it may be self-evident upon reflection that this process is necessary.   Energy must have that which is to be energised, light acquires significance from darkness, and virtue from sin, and so on through all the forms under which the polarity appears.

Here it is our concern to speak of human psychology, of man's inner life and its outward expression. The result of this dichotomy or twofold cleavage in the stream of life, is a type-differentiation of so profound a character that, were it not overlaid in individual cases by the almost infinite complexity of human nature, it could not escape the attention of any student thereof, however superficially minded.

Man, even corporeally considered, is a unity. The fact that he can will, feel and reason as an individual, establishes this. If this fact of unity becomes obscured in particular cases or special circumstances (as in the drunkard's inability to co-ordinate his movements) the result is immediately recognised as pathological and abnormal. All effective and intelligent living depends upon the control exercised by this unitary principle in man over the diverse faculties, the different limbs, the organs of the body and the emotions and impulses. Most of us become conscious, if we withdraw into ourselves, of a " dweller in the inmost " that can, as it were, stand apart and watch, and even judge, the activities of the personality which surrounds it, remaining in itself exempt and transcendent in respect of them. This unitary principle is said by the psycho-analysts to appear in dreams as a monarch, prince or chieftain, naturally suggesting to the astrologer the Sun.

From the standpoint of this dweller within all but itself is circumstance. Even the thoughts and instincts, and still more the acts, of its own personality are environmental to it. So, too, the body, and all the terrestrial associations of the personality with other personalities, with their operations, and with the world of nature.

It can and does distinguish between its thoughts and emotions which it can in some degree control and the more remote environment over which it has far less mastery, verging to that region which is so far beyond its influence that it may be called the domain of Fate, of Adrasteia, the Unescapable.

Some find the interior world of thought and impulse harder to control than the exterior fields. Men may win battles but be quite unable to dominate their own instincts. But fundamentally there is always this dweller within and the world of circumstance without.

Now we return to our two types, positive and negative.

We find that the ego, when brought into relation with the external world, has the choice of two reactions. These correspond to the active and passive types. He may attempt to master it for his own ends, or he may submit to it.

How many great thinkers have wrestled with this problem !

The " man in the street " has his own philosophy, embodied in a hundred proverbs.

In the main the man of science tries to understand and utilise Nature and to improve living conditions, and most " practical men " belong to the same school. On the other hand religionists and philosophers have tended to teach resignation, renunciation and endurance or else have sought by metaphysical argument to persuade us the external does not really exist, that it is an illusion, or at any rate something very different from what it appears to be.

Astrology, being integral in its outlook, allows for both points of view. It applauds those who seek to conquer nature, but it recognises also the existence of the unsurmountable, at least at the present time and in particular circumstances. What futurity may behold in the way of achievement is another matter. The positive signs are the fighters, the negative the yielders, or shall we rather say, those who fight the defensive battles?

For we must not, in astrology, fall into the obvious trap of identifying the positive with the Good and the negative with the Evil. We have indeed given some examples of polaritic thinking that might seem to justify this error. But in true astrology this correspondence must not be carried too far. We recognise the distinctive virtues and failings of both types. We assign its place to each. Probably we believe that an harmonious mixture is, except for special tasks, the best.

Does astrology, in truth, admit anything as essentially evil?

The answer must depend upon one's philosophical conceptions. Many maps unquestionably indicate *difficult* lives, and these difficulties may be such as to make life not only a hard struggle with external circumstances, but also apt to produce conflict with accepted moral usages and standards, i.e., in theological language, a liability to grave temptations to sin. This, as astrologers, we know and the knowledge should make for understanding. How we interpret the fact is another matter.

In practical horoscopy a positive map contains many bodies in positive signs, with the ascendant also positive, whilst the Sun, Mars, Jupiter, Uranus and perhaps Pluto may all be reckoned as positivising influences. On the other hand, many bodies in negatives and prominence of the Moon, Venus and Neptune incline to the passive attitude. Mercury tends to the positive, though it is adaptable and in that sense yielding. Saturn, from this point of view, is hard to classify : perhaps, with its exaltation in the Scales, at the midpoint of the zodiac, it represents the synthesis of both types, prudent in defence yet active in its slow, patient way. It is the wise planet ; it sees the need of both values.

Thus, as we have said, the active type has as its aim the subjection of the external to itself and the making of its life what it wills that this should be. Hence it is prone to be aggressive, dominating, hopeful, aspiring and full of desire.

The statesman is the type of the man who wishes to mould other human beings to his will. Scientists, engineers and agriculturalists show the same tendency as directed towards nature.

The active type is always progressive and hopeful of better things. It takes risks readily and may degenerate into the gambler, for one of its common weaknesses is a lack of patience which tries to get quick results. Further, its optimism may cause it to ignore obvious hard fact. It may overstep social and moral laws and develop along the familiar lines of *Hubris*, self-willed arrogance and pride.

These are characteristic of some phases of positive-emotion, the element of Fire.

But the positive-air type is also active on lines of mental construction. It seeks to control the external through work in the study or laboratory.

A common development of the positive intellectual type follows the line that the unpleasant aspects of the outer world are non-existent. This belief, which receives so many jolts in our day-to-day experiences, sometimes pursues a religious course of argument, those who hold it affirming

that since God is good and created all things, every
created thing and condition must also be perfectly good,
whatever our senses may testify. In this type the normal
struggle with the objective becomes an interior struggle
between what is regarded as Divine Truth and " mortal
mind."

Mrs. Mary Baker Eddy's hour of birth is unrecorded,
but she was born on 16 July, 1821, and we are at once
struck by the characteristic Sun square Saturn-Jupiter.
Aquarius is a not unlikely ascendant, which would place the
Sun in the 6th house, with the affairs of which her teachings
have had so much to do, whilst the conjunction of the two
major planets might fall in the 2nd or 3rd houses, probably
the former. Such a stress, from 6th to 2nd, would show a
bitter sense of frustration in regard to material limitations,
and particularly those of worldly means and bodily
health, and Jupiter, while it would strive to help, would be
impeded by the square and indicate religious doubts and
difficulties. Powerful trines from another conjunction, of
Uranus and Neptune to Saturn-Jupiter, produced a
solution, presumably satisfactory to Mrs. Eddy as it has
been to many thousands of her disciples, of a transcendental character in keeping with the nature of the two
helping planets.

We need not pause to ask how, if everything is perfect,
mortal mind has been able to obtrude its delusions. More
classical philosophers have sought heroically to demonstrate that everything is for the best in the best possible
of worlds but this is hardly the place to examine their
theories. Most people will agree that there appears to be
room for improvement and it is the business of the
astrologer to help himself and others towards a fuller
understanding and enjoyment of life.

A frequent attitude is the typically Saturnian one of
duty. Here, so to speak, the sufferer seeks help from a hair

of the dog that bit him. Saturn, which signifies so many
of our griefs and troubles, bids us do our duty and rest
satisfied, without indulging in metaphysical speculation.

The (debased) Epicureanism that tells us to enjoy all we
can and live for the present seems allied to the benefic
planets, in their least noble manifestation.

All the systems that stress the idea of *karma* are
Saturnian, involving the conception of strict justice. They
suffer from the fact that they almost destroy the possibility
of disinterested beneficence ; and the same is true of those
presentations of Christianity which stress the notion of
future rewards and punishments.

However, the trait that all positive forms have in
common is their refusal merely to accept the external
world *passively*. They are acutely conscious of the existence of a Not-Self that is, at least in appearance, other
than they wish it to be, and they seek a solution of the
stress actively, whether by action, in thought, or
emotionally.

But with the passive type the attitude of the ego
towards the external is one of submission, of acquiescence.
It does not seek to alter what is outside itself but takes
things as it finds them and rather tries to change itself
to their mould.   " He hath an understanding of things
divine who hath nobly agreed with Necessity," said the
Stoic. But the passive person tends to regard too many
things as belonging to the realm of the necessary and
foreordained ; he does not merely say " what can't
be cured must be endured " but prefers to endure many
things that a balanced type would succeed in altering and
improving.

He " takes things as he finds them." He desires not to
win the new, but to preserve the old ; he is timid and
prudent rather than venturesome and explorative, preferring a mediocre known to a dangerous if glorious

unknown. " Things are best as they are " ; he " lets well alone," dislikes " new-fangled " things, and says that what was good enough for mother is good enough for him.

This class is not necessarily less intelligent than the positives. It will often be more so, at least in terms of erudition and book-learning. For, shirking a developed outer life, it may do much to unfold the inner faculties. What it lacks is actual experience and living contacts.

Dr. Richard Garnett, the librarian of the British Museum, had the " Four Principals " (Sun, Moon, ruler and ascendant) in negative signs, as well as two other bodies. Because of their prudential tendency the negatives are often great collectors and hoarders, and this propensity may exhibit itself over a wide range of objects, from collecting stamps, to share-certificates, and to the accumulation of factual knowledge. It is not only denoted by many planets in negative signs ; in its acute form it is more often shown by Moon-Saturn contacts. But these, essentially, have a similar significance to that of negative overstress in terms of the signs.

These people may study both man and nature, but more often the latter. It does not view it as something to be used, but as something to be admired and loved for its own sake, for what it is. It listens to the voice of nature ; it does not read itself into it.

Insofar as it is active—and obviously it cannot avoid action altogether so long as it is alive, even if it lives in a hermit's cell—it is active in defence, not in aggression. In this sense it will fight tenaciously, as is evinced by the history of Cancer nations, such as the Dutch, both in their homeland and in South Africa.

To the positive the Self is the supreme fact and all else is a mere fringe around it, but to the negative the exterior is something which must be constantly and anxiously watched, if possible from the comparative safety of home and hearth.

It is clear that what is popularly called escapism, in its innumerable forms, belongs to the negatives ; and in particular the escape from actuality into the kingdoms of fantasy—in other words, day-dreaming—is a negative habit, particularly allied to the element Water in conjunction with Air. In this way the obstacles that actual life presents are avoided and an imaginary Paradise is constructed, in which the ego can picture itself freely in any guise that appeals to it, as a saint, a king, a conqueror, a statesman and so forth. Naturally such indulgences can lead to deplorable results, when, for example, the phantast loses touch with actuality altogether and becomes convinced that he is some mighty or famous being. But whether a mild tendency to them is serious is debatable.

Drug-taking and alcoholism are methods of obtaining an illusory sense of adequacy. The overnegative type is aware of his defects, his inability to cope with actual life ; drink makes him feel, temporarily, equal to his tasks. For, of course, few people are in a position to live in permanent seclusion. But it would be unwise to say that all alcoholic excess is of this category.

Fatalism is commonly found among the negatives, for this standpoint excuses them from the responsibility of vigorous action :   it is all preordained, so why trouble ?

Negatives are often very happy with their books, allotments, gardens, and home hobbies ; but life is always apt to force them into contact with the surge of circumstances that they would gladly shun.

As a rule the Negative is trustworthy, for he has no inner urge to be freakish or erratic. Dishonesty is a risky adventure and such exploits are not to his taste. If he is a criminal, it is usually because he has been led astray by other more enterprising types.

There is a strong protective element in the passive composition. It is more patient, more understanding and more sympathetic than the active polarity, although again, because it is self-protective, it can be a convinced believer in the adage that charity begins at home.

Great love of animals is common. For the animal kingdom, on the whole, occupies a passive position *vis-à-vis* of man and is largely at his mercy. Miss Lind-af-Hageby, the well-known anti-vivisectionist, has Sun, Moon and every planet in negative signs.

Sex is the supreme exemplification of the principle of polarity and the sexual act is the consummation of the fusion between the two poles, on the physical level. But many men are born with negative genitures, and conversely.

Dr. Jung, in *Psychological Types*, deals with the early Christian fathers Origen and Tertullian in a manner that is of great interest in this connection. The former emasculated himself in order to silence the clamours of the body and render himself the better able to receive the divine influx. Thus he sought, by a surgical operation, to change his polarity. Tertullian, by training a lawyer, strove to pass beyond the limits imposed by his intellectual acumen and logical sense in the statement that the resurrection was "certain because impossible." We may say, astrologically, the Origen tried to excise the Fire-element from his nature and Tertullian sought to banish that of Air and Earth—reason and common-sense. Christianity, largely a Water-religion, has often found itself in conflict with the values represented by Fire (in its common form, animal spirits) and Air (philosophical reasoning).

Both the Fathers took the view that one part of our nature must be renounced for the sake of another. Astrology admits ordinate and inordinate manifestations of all its values but refuses to judge any of them to be essentially bad. On the contrary, careful examination will show that they are all necessary. The goal is ordination and integration.

In passing we note that self-castration was also performed by the pagan worshippers of the Great Mother, the symbol of the passive principle.

The assault on the sexual organs is an obvious way of attempting to subject the naturally dominant active part to the naturally subservient passive principle. But a great many less easily understood practices are really aimed at the same result. For example, religious fasting, which subdues the animal spirits and is supposed to render the subject more capable of receiving supernal illuminations.

The dislike of reason is common to many of the passive types. For reason is essentially an active principle ; indeed, all thought is necessarily an activity. Reason is also a limitation ; it obeys laws and depends upon exact definition of terms. Therefore it is contrary to the characteristics of the emotional man, for the feelings know no laws. Hence the passive-emotional type, symbolised in astrology by the element of Water, is most of all averse to reason ; but Fire also insists on a freer expression than logical thought will permit.

Thus we find William Blake (Ascendant and Moon in Cancer, Sun in Sagittarius) regarding reason as a principle of death. It is true that a predominance of the analytical and sceptical forms of mental activity leads to a dead end.

Blake wrote :

> " If the sun and moon should doubt
> They'd immediately go out."

In the Upanishads we read that " the mind is the slayer of the real " and the medieval mystic wrote " By love He may be gotten and holden, but by thought never." Such sentiments represent the revolt against the tyranny of Air. Our science accords them some justification, for we have always given Fire a certain priority amongst the Elements.

It is interesting to note that both active and passive methods of achieving racial survival occur in very easily recognised forms.

For example, the ferocity of the carnivora is essentially of the positive category and to the same class we may relate the skill shown by certain animals in a high degree in hunting and finding food.

Typical passive methods are flight, camouflage, protective armour and sheer bulk.

Another protection to the race is extreme prolificness, in which both positive and negative polarities are involved.

It is by his mental powers that man has attained his present domination over the globe. He has not the teeth or claws of the carnivora, the armour and thick hide of the crocodile and rhinoceros, he is not prolific, he has not the speed in flight of the deer or birds. But he has invented weapons a thousand times more destructive than claw or tooth, he has made himself armour of steel, and he has manufactured machines that surpass any animal in their rapidity and endurance. He tries to compensate poor proliferation by means of infant welfare clinics. He seeks artificial protection from the weather by means of clothing and homes and invents special foods that are supposed, by some, to possess virtues unknown to natural products.

The solution of the polarity-conflict on the bodily plane in sex is achieved more or less satisfactorily by most human beings, but the psychological problem is not so easily dealt with. Physically all normal human beings are male or female, but psychologically there are all sorts of degrees and variations. Every man has a Moon in his horoscope ; every woman has a Sun, and so forth. If the geniture shows a sharp conflict of polarity, tension cannot be escaped. Wedded partnerships can be dissolved but the inner struggle must either be resolved or continue until the final triumph of the negative principle, so far as the body goes, in death. To achieve a complete life the two poles must either be fused or at least taught to operate in concord.

Some might ask whether the conflict of polarities is necessarily evil ? There are those who believe in war and tension. It seems that a complete failure to reconcile the Opposites would rend the nature asunder in insanity or death ; but there is truth in the aphorism of Heracleitus that "strife is the parent of all things." This applies equally to the stresses of " malefic " aspects, which do not always indicate a polarity-tension.

Tension breeds activity and entire harmonisation tends to repose and stagnation. One of the first lessons that an intelligent student learns is that he cannot classify nativities as good and bad by adding up the number of allegedly benefic and malefic aspects.

The problem involves the philosophy of life which any particular individual may adopt. In other words, what does he mean by " good " and " bad " ? This we cannot answer for him ; but it seems a fact that most of those whom the generality of mankind acclaim as " great " or even as " successful " have mixed figures of birth. Constructive aspects showing their powers of achievement ; obstructive formation showing the difficulties they had to surmount in order to win their titles to applause. Very harmonious nativities do not seek to perform deeds of derring-do ; they are quite happy as they are. Very discordant maps are usually too much at variance with their circumstances (and often within themselves) to attain really lasting and useful results. At best their achievements are temporary and tainted with extremism.

Nevertheless it may be admitted that when the social structure has degenerated to such an extent that violent measures are necessary, then violent nativities may also be required to cleanse the Augean stables. Thus the horoscope of Lenin* is mainly one of severe stress, though not entirely so. That of Gandhi shows a blend of the tensive and constructive values.

Some readers, presumably of the negative type, will perhaps regard the picture of stress and difficult reconciliation as depressing.

Perhaps it is, at least for this class.

But there appears to be a tendency in nature to establish a certain degree of working balance even when the natus is difficult. The same pessimism may seem to be justified by the fact that we have more " bad " aspects and planets than " good " ones. But here again the answer seems to be that the *background* of life is at least reasonably enjoyable.

During by far the greater part of our lives we are not directly feeling the impact of any of our horoscopic formations, harmonious or discordant. The clear and unmistakable obtrusion into our consciousness of our " afflictions " is episodic rather than perpetual, except of course in cases of chronic disease or disablement. Some, like Pope, must talk of " this long disease my life." Theirs is a pitiable lot but even Pope had his compensations. For the most part we find that, as the body, when given fair play, reverts after disease to some kind of normal functioning, so, too, do our affairs. Young people fancy that their emotional troubles are of the nature of major tragedies ; but in time they learn better.

The work of the astrologer is to guide and direct. He

*All nativities quoted in this work without data may be found in *1001 Notable Nativities* or in the two additional booklets compiled by Maurice Wemyss and entitled *More Notable Nativities* and *Famous Nativities*. Some are in varying degrees hypothetical.

sees when and where progress is possible ; when and where frustration is at hand.

Another helpful fact is that we are affected by the nativities of those whom we contact. We will not go to the absurd extreme of one writer who claimed that sexual intercourse fused the nativities of the participating couple, so that for the rest of their lives each bore the geniture of the other superimposed upon his or her own, nor need we speculate as to what the horoscopic condition of, let us say, Nero must have been on this supposition towards the close of his life. But the man or woman who lacks " Fire " can secure compensation *via* the companionship of a Fire-element friend, and so on with all types.

It may be argued that it is best for a strongly developed type, be it positive or negative, to activate as that type and not to endeavour to become something different from what he is " meant to be." Here once more it is a question of individual outlook. But it can probably be affirmed with safety that *at least* an understanding of other types and a certain degree of sympathy and rapprochement should be sought.

CHAPTER V

ASPECTS IN TERMS OF THE SIGNS

TEXTBOOKS commonly deal with the various aspects between bodies. But, perforce, they leave the student to consider for himself what modification will be introduced into the textbook descriptions by the signs which the aspecting planets, in each particular instance, may occupy.

A book that contained every possible aspect in every possible sign-combination would be, of course, almost inconceivable. And even this would not be final, by any means. For though I might by diligent search find, let us say, twenty examples of Sun trine Mars, Aries to Leo, yet these twenty cases would not be in the least comparable. *No aspect can really be abstracted from the horoscope to which it belongs and treated as self-existent.* Such abstractions are made—our textbooks consist of little else. But all must recognise that they are in the highest degree artificial and correspond to nothing in Nature. Their excuse is that nothing else is humanly possible.

In this Chapter the design is to reverse the usual procedure, and, instead of treating the planetary contacts without reference to the signs, to treat aspects in terms of the signs without referring, except incidentally, to the planets that may be involved.

And it is believed that this approach will be found to be informative and worth while. If all aspects between Sun and Mars, for example, will be discovered upon examination to have something in common, irrespective of whether they fall in the fire, air, earth or water triplicities, so it is claimed that all aspects between let us say Aries and Leo, or any other two signs, will have a common element in their significance, irrespective of the bodies forming them. Naturally this common element will be affected, and often largely obscured, by the qualities of the bodies ; but it will still be there.

In examining the signs, preparatory to this work, we have to note their various classifications.

We have already dealt with that of Positive and Negative.

There is the tendency of the first two or three to crudity and practicality and the corresponding propensity of the last two or three to idealism.

There is the distinction between the limited scope of the first six and the expanded expression of the second six, of which more in a later chapter.

Furthermore, there is the division into three Quadruplicities.

There are the four Triplicities or symbolic Elements.

There is the division, not so often noticed and yet very important, between the Fire and the Water signs ruled by the Lights, Jupiter and Mars, on the one hand, and, on the other hand, the Air and Earth signs ruled by Mercury, Venus and Saturn. We have no name for this division or for Fire-Water in contrast to Air-Earth, but the contrast is real and important. Fire and Water are emotional ; Air and Earth mental. In each case the positive is upward-tending or anabasic and the negative is downward-tending or catabasic.

Fire symbolises at its lowest level animal spirits ; thence it moves up the scale of manifestation to aspiration and (combined with Air) the creative imagination. Water exhibits its quality in forms to which we apply such words as moods and humours, the personal and downward-tending passions and desires.

If, emotionally, we can relate Fire to joy, so we must link Water with sorrow. We might go further and claim that they have, respectively, an affinity with Life and Death.

The two principles are well portrayed in Tennyson's poem "The Two Voices." They are the spirit that affirms and the spirit that denies.

But, as we must emphasise, there is in Nature a movement towards the normal which compensates for excessive tendencies in one direction. Fire, despite its glorious uprush of vivid life, can collapse badly. Water, for all its melancholic proclivity, may exhibit tenacity and patient endurance. Not all suicides, for example, are of the Water type

Morally, too, Fire may be careless of others or at least lack understanding, whereas Water will show sympathy and understanding

In the practical life Fire is apt to be too venturesome and Water too timid, yet, because of its very weakness, the latter can be shrewd and discerning, prudent and forethoughtful.

If these two elements are strong, to the detriment of the Air-Earth representation, the nature is obviously over-prone to emotionalism.

Air is, in its highest manifestation, pure intellect and (combined with Fire) creative imagination. In lower types it inclines to useless day-dreaming and indolence but is associative, friendly and harmless, without depth of feeling.

Earth is the practical mind, which in its lower expressions tends, like Air, to be lazy, and also to be coarse, narrow-minded and stupid.

We will now consider the significance of the various combinations of the signs when linked by aspect, beginning with the eighteen possible sign-contacts that arise by square and opposition. There are six groups, each with three specific types :

Thus,

1. Fire square Water
$$\left\{\begin{array}{l} ♈—♋ \\ ♌—♏ \\ ♐—♓ \end{array}\right.$$

2. Earth square Air
$$\left\{\begin{array}{l} ♉—♒ \\ ♍—♊ \\ ♑—♎ \end{array}\right.$$

3. Fire square Earth
$$\left\{\begin{array}{l} ♈—♑ \\ ♌—♉ \\ ♐—♍ \end{array}\right.$$

4. Air square Water
$$\left\{\begin{array}{l} ♊—♓ \\ ♎—♋ \\ ♒—♏ \end{array}\right.$$

5. Fire opposition Air
$$\left\{\begin{array}{l} ♈—♎ \\ ♌—♒ \\ ♐—♊ \end{array}\right.$$

6. Earth opposition Water
$$\left\{\begin{array}{l} ♉—♏ \\ ♍—♓ \\ ♑—♋ \end{array}\right.$$

(1) Squares between bodies in Fire and Water generate great strength, even violence, and are potential sources of tragedy. Yet they occur frequently in the genitures of successful and gifted men. One does not need to look far, in a collection of the maps of famous people, to find examples of this type.

The propensity to excessive feeling may surge up into uncontrollable anger or virtuous indignation, or it may decline into sentimentality.

(*a*) Aries-Cancer.   This is represented by Annie

Besant, the "passionate pilgrim," Isadora Duncan, the classic dancer, Mrs. Eddy, Von Keyserling, the German philosopher, G. B. Shaw, and Gandhi. It might be called the square of the stormy petrel.

(*b*) Leo-Scorpio. This seems much less often present in maps of the famous. It is potentially a difficult emplacement for the square contact. It may nourish bitterness, soured by the memory of ancient wrongs ; it may be vindictive ; the emotional life will be swept by penetrating grief. It would make a good position for a satirist ; indeed we find that it is present in the natus of William Blake, who wrote some mordant lines. The fixed nature of the signs congeals and deepens the feelings.

(*c*) Sagittarius-Pisces. By reason of the mutable " sattvic " nature of the signs, this presents a much less difficult problem. There is likely to be excess of feeling and sentiment, with emotional restlessness, particularly about problems of the intellect. It is, because both signs are Jovian, prone to prodigality.

Cases are—King Edward VII, Chopin, P. B. Das, Indian anarchist, and Vaillant, French anarchist, Charles Dickens, Thomas Hardy, Sir Isaac Newton.

A careful study of these examples will show how the characteristics of the formation worked out ; sometimes it is all too obvious. But it seems undeniable that such squares are far from hostile to success. As we have said, they generate power.

So much for Fire-Water interplay.

(2) As we have said, both Air and Earth relate to the mental life, to thought.

(*a*) Taurus-Aquarius exhibits the contrast between a socially-minded and idealistic attitude and a self-regarding one. Persons whose genitures show this type of square are often engaged on commerce or finance

on the one hand and on scientific pursuits or philanthropy on the other. One calls to mind Lord Avebury
(Sir John Lubbock) the banker, archaeologist and
naturalist, and on referring to the positions on his
birthday (30 April, 1834) the author was interested to
find that he had the Sun in Taurus and the Moon in
Aquarius. The combination does not seem to produce
strong psychological stress and some might regard the
division of interests as adding to the pleasures of life (on
which subject Lord Avebury wrote a book) rather than
detracting from them. Air is an accommodating and
normalising influence.

Disabling physical precipitation may be present ; and
as an example in point we may quote the natus of
Franklin D. Roosevelt, where, however, the afflictions
are notably severe. The native's desire to better the
material conditions (Taurus) of the people (Aquarius)
is true to this type. Lord Avebury instituted bank
holidays in Britain.

At best this combination stands for practical idealism,
or science and sense.

It may be observed (though we shall revert to the
point at a later stage) that Aquarius stands for the so-
called herd-instinct, or gregarious aspect of human life.
Hence afflictions that involve this sign denote either
that the native is unable to adapt himself to social life
or that the social life around him for some reason rejects
him. And conversely when the sign is harmoniously
integrated with the horoscope.

It will be clear that none of the Earth-Air squares are as
difficult in their nature as those between Fire and Water.

(b) Virgo-Gemini : Here we have two signs both
common in nature and ruled by the same planet, and
the squares here are also less dangerous than many,
though they may produce discontent, due to the frustra-

tion of the higher Element Air by the lower Earth, and this may manifest as a captious attitude, hard to please and given to bitter feelings and remarks. The square usually generates high mental activity and intelligence of no mean order, though there may be physical indolence.

Perhaps one of the main weaknesses of the class is lack of incentive ; they are apt to find nothing worth while. There is a tendency to bookishness and seclusion.

Naturally much must depend on the strength of Mercury in cases such as these. If it is severely afflicted, dishonesty and sharp practice may occur.

(c) Capricorn-Libra : This type tends to polish, gravity and a certain aloofness. It would befit a statesman, diplomat or professional man, particularly a specialist.

Curiously enough it occurs in the birth-figures both of Gladstone and Disraeli.

It is the very antithesis of the Aries-Cancer square (as might be expected) ; here there is no Berserk rage, but a cool and collected attitude, seemingly detached but actually watching all things carefully. It would be the perfect civil servant, at least as Tallyrand defined him " completely efficient and entirely devoid of zeal."

We have now discussed the contacts between Elements which belong to the same one of the two primary divisions of the zodiac. That is, between Fire-Water (both emotional) and between Air-Earth (both mental). We come next to those conflicts which cut across this division, that is, between Fire and Earth and between Air and Water. These, of course, are basically different in their nature. Those that we have already dealt with tend to be *exaggerative* in character ; they lead to excess of emotion or of mind. In the class we shall now discuss mind and emotion directly clash ; we do not find an exaggeration of either, but a struggle for mastery between the two.

(3) Fire square Earth seems an obviously difficult combination.

It is pre-eminently the *square of objective frustration*, of not getting what you want. The emotional nature, the desires, meet here the solid facts of the objective world which say " Nay " to them. If the signs are occupied by bodies of like nature (as for example the Sun in Fire and Saturn in Earth) then the effects will of course be all the clearer and more drastic—this point applies, one need hardly say, to all these studies.

It is, therefore, the quadrature of hard struggle. We find it, for instance, in the cases of J. M. Barrie and the great Hahnemann, and, quite strongly, in Adolf Hitler, who had an earthly planet (Saturn) in Fire and a fiery planet (Mars) in Earth. Indeed it is present in Winston Churchill's map— Moon in Virgo square Sun in Sagittarius. It brought the pride of Louis XIV (Mercury in Virgo square Mars in Sagittarius) into difficulties.

It will be seen that this formation does not necessarily spell defeat, either interior or exterior. As regards the former, we refer to a nativity that was made the subject of a competition in " Astrology " for December, 1944. The native was born at Weymouth, Dorsetshire, on 1 August, 1864, at 00.30 a.m. Here Sun in Leo is square two planets in Taurus. She voluntarily and cheerfully forsook town life and lived in circumstances of extreme hardship all her life—and thoroughly enjoyed them. Thus free will enters in ; we cannot alter the main lines of our nativities, but we can certainly follow them readily or reluctantly according to our own determination. It is true that the " main lines " of our psychological qualities are also indicated by the horoscope of birth. Jupiter in Sagittarius is not Saturn in Capricorn ; but there is an ordinate, as opposed to an inordinate, expression of both values.

A digression on Fate and Free will is hardly out of place here, for the Fire-Earth conflict is precisely concerned with this problem. It comes to a head here, and those who meditate deeply on it (and the philosophic astrologer can hardly avoid doing so) often have the related stress in their maps. One could quote Alan Leo again in this connection.

A " Young Spendthrift " (*Notable Nativities*, No. 260) who regarded himself as *fated* to waste his substance had, most appropriately, the Sun in Aries square Saturn in Capricorn.

Those who are confronted with the Fire-Earth problem, then, must expect obstruction to their life-expression. They need not, however, react in the idiotic manner that served this man for an excuse. They will rather decide, carefully and patiently, what they may wisely expect to obtain from life, and they will then accept the results of their efforts with good heart. Each case will vary, according to the bodies involved, the houses occupied, and the rest of the horoscope. The woman cited above had a free outlet for her afflicted Sun in a close trine of that luminary to Neptune. Others are not so fortunate. Had she set her heart on wealth, she would inevitably have been defeated, for the squares from Taurus must have proved too strong.

The extravagance of N.N. No. 260 was an act of silly bravado, as if one could prove one's indifference to Earth-limitation by flinging away what one has.

To take the Fire-Earth type under its three heads, we will begin with.

(*a*) the Aries-Capricorn square, which, in contrast to the Capricorn-Libra class, has an undercurrent of selfishness and tends to roughness and violence, as for example the case of the mass-murderer Kuerten (born 3.30 a.m., 26 May, 1883, at Cologne) and *Notable Nativities* Nos. 56, 560 and 764.

It is less excitable than Aries-Cancer, but more cunning. It would probably find its best expression in some occupation involving skill in action with a modicum of difficulty and danger, as a life at sea or in pioneer colonisation. It would rebel strongly against a humdrum life.

(*b*) Leo-Taurus has violent possibilities, often with a motive of monetary gain. Landru, for instance, the French Bluebeard, had Pluto rising in Taurus in square to Mars in Leo. But the " incorruptible " Robespierre had Sun in Taurus square Neptune and Mars in Leo.

One might expect a strongly speculative element here in finance. There would be great stubbornness and probable pride.

Physical precipitation in the form of obstinate disease is likely. There is also the liability to emotional sorrows.

(*c*) Sagittarius-Virgo is a typically critical combination, Virgo striving to reduce to precise order and expression the ideas that the fiery sign perpetually throws off in the course of its intellectual explorings. It is unlikely to be a dangerous contact unless violent bodies are implicated ; it will disperse its force in debate and disputation.

It is the sort of square one would expect to find in the maps of enthusiasts for theological controversy, and Henry VIII, who took his share in that form of activity, so much in vogue in his time, had a square in these signs, joined with that typically theological position, Jupiter in Gemini. His use of religious qualms in the matter of obtaining his divorce seems well in agreement with the square between the self-regarding Virgo and Sagittarius. His daughter Elizabeth had a similar configuration.

(4) We come next to Air square Water, a conflict which is frequently productive of unhealthy mental conditions, including phobias, or irrational fears. This relationship is not difficult to understand. There is the impact between the reasoning mind and the all-various contents of the subconscious, with which Water is closely connected. So little kinship or resemblance is there between these two elements that difficulties of the above kind are sure to arise. It is like wedding a sylph, a delicate spirit of the Air, with a will-o'-the-wisp which is the unwholesome product of marsh and swamp. Reconciliation is impossible; disentanglement is difficult. Only the perpetual effort of nature to normalise, assisted by skilled psychological treatment, may avail to resolve the knots, or so-called complexes, that will appear. Vague fears, derived perhaps from remote experiences of the brain-cells in far-back ancestors, perhaps from shocks in infancy, or possibly from something as prosaic as gastric or hepatic trouble, creep towards and seek to derange the pure action of thought and reason.

If Fire-Earth represents the struggle between the will and the hard resistance of actuality, so this type stands for the struggle between reason and the irrational, mental order against the chaos of the unconscious. Much, as always, must depend upon the bodies involved in each particular example, but the underlying condition, shown by the signs, the essential background, is this.

(a) It may be proposed that the Gemini-Pisces square is less serious because the common signs have always a possibility of dispelling their difficulties in talk and discussion, and the fixed embedded quality of the usual " complex " is most likely to occur under the fixed signs. But circumstances arise when talk is impossible, viz., in solitude, and the author has bad cases of phobic dread of solitude (and of the dark—symbolical of negativity) under this square. Fear of insanity may also occur. I have also an example of obsession by a negro (again a symbol of the negative). The Empress of Mexico, who lost her reason after her husband's execution and developed a dread of poison, had this square, combined with other extremely heavy stresses.

All forms of fear are exaggerated if Saturn, who has his detriment in Cancer, the prime Water sign, is implicated.

At best this type would probably tend to superficial chatter and restlessness of mind and body, with a good deal of general kindliness. For it may be said that almost any Piscean factor—and this includes Neptune—operates against harshness and roughness.

(b) The Libra-Cancer inhibitions are likely to affect *action*. Stage-fright is a good example, shyness another. The latter is a general condition arising in the presence of strangers ; the former occurs in more special circumstances. Both arise from a sense of inadequacy which in certain situations paralyses the power to act, even when the reason assures the sufferer that there is nothing to fear. It seems as if the will is unable to exert its normal powers ; there are some things which the native, though perhaps usually a quite normal person, " can't face."

That human beings, especially those brought up in large towns, should have a propensity towards this sort of inhibition, does not seem at all strange. Most of us are mere ciphers amongst thousands of others. As children we are dependent upon our parents, as employees upon our employer, in old age upon the kindness or even charity of others. Thus many live in a state of conscious fear and anxiety, whilst in others the conscious mind rejects these states, only to repress them into the subconscious, whence they arise sooner or later disguised in some form which only the insight of a student of such matters will detect.

Nevertheless normally human nature reacts healthily to these facts and most people, perhaps, are able to find for themselves a position in life which they can fill to their own reasonable satisfaction. But when the calling is unwisely chosen or when destiny is particularly cruel, the victim may lose all confidence in himself and all hope and courage ; or he may develop some phobic inhibition, which will affect him only in specific conditions more or less plainly shown in the nativity.

If the Fire-Earth native cannot *get* what he wants, the Air-Water subject cannot *do* (or perhaps more properly, *will* to do) what he wishes.

However, lest it be thought too gloomy a picture has been painted, it may be recalled that Libra is a highly normalising sign and Cancer by no means a dangerous one, so that bad cases are uncommon, though it is probable that more exist than is generally believed.

In any severe case of unbalance it is very rarely one planetary contact alone that is to be blamed.

(c) Aquarius-Scorpio indicates a difficulty in *social* self-expression through physical or psychological defect or deficiency. In one case of this type the native was so shy as to be unable to " dine out." Charles Darwin was in the same predicament ; his nervousness in these circumstances, produced vomiting. His time of birth is, so far as the writer knows, unrecorded but he had the Sun in Aquarius parallel Uranus in Scorpio (born 12 February, 1809).

Thus while the Libra-Cancer native may wish to shun positions in which he is conspicuous (stage-fright), the present category dislikes immersion in social assemblies. It is well known to homeopaths that some neurotic patients are best in company; others the reverse. Scorpio is naturally a solitary sign, Aquarius a gregarious one; here the two tendencies are in conflict. The aloofness of the Victorian and post-Victorian Englishman may be indicated by the square of the ruler in Aquarius to Neptune (a shy planet) in Scorpio in our 1801 map. It does not seem that this unfortunate national trait came into evidence before the 19th century.

In extreme forms (and it is these we must study as best illustrating the principles concerned) it is clear that we may find a genuine hatred (Scorpio) of the human race (Aquarius); a fierce rejection of the fact of man's gregarious nature and its natural consequences and responsibilities.

Thus, extreme cases of this type produce the *indiscriminate* homicide or mass-murderer.

In ordinary cases the manifestation will probably take the form of marked shyness or uneasiness in the presence of unfamiliar people. Sometimes there will be unconventional habits and a cult of " being different " from other people which is an expression, partly unconscious, of disapproval.

On the other hand, if " strong " planets are involved, there may be a reaction from shyness that will manifest as boastfulness, swagger or a habit of sarcasm.

Since fixed signs are concerned, these traits are not easy to displace, but the tendency might be sublimated in some such occupation as surgery or in the military services.

We come now to two classes of opposition, those between Fire and Air and those between Water and Earth. Each of these has as complements the sextiles between the same

Elements, which indicate their harmonious functioning, but even the oppositions should not present an impossible problem in reconciliation since the Elements concerned are not hostile.

(5) Fire and Air, opposed, indicate a tension between the aspirations and the reason, and, since at their higher levels, these should not be in conflict, there seems no basis for supposing that an irreconcilable struggle need arise. It is true that at lower levels one may find the usual signs of an opposition, such as separations; but it will also often be found upon examination that these have not had a permanently injurious effect. One may instance Dr. Annie Besant's separation from her husband and the secessions that took place in the Theosophical Society under her presidency. In a sense such things can be be rightly regarded as of the nature of " growing pains."

(a) The first opposition—Aries to Libra—is exemplified in her case. In Nietzsche's horoscope we find an opposition of the same planets (Mercury and Uranus) in the same signs, assisted indeed by strong mediation, i.e., bodies in sextile and trine to the two planets in opposition. He, too, was something of a " passionate pilgrim " and one may ask why did he lose his reason, whilst Dr. Besant, even if some of her enthusiasms met with widespread incredulity, most certainly retained her reason to the end ? To this question one could reply at some length. For one thing, Aries is much less liable to deep psychological unrest than is Scorpio ; further, the philosopher's Mercury was involved in an affliction from Neptune in the 3rd house, whereas Dr. Besant's Mercury had the conjunction of Venus and the contact, albeit a square, of an exalted Jupiter.

Still, both cases show the possibility of the speculative element breaking away from the restraint of Air. Yet in both, failure, if failure there was, had the stamp of noble endeavour upon it. There is usually something fine, in greater or less degree, in Fire-Air conflicts.

(b) Leo-Aquarius oppositions have produced great men, distinguished for courage and endurance. Leaders (Leo) of men (Aquarius) in difficult circumstances (the opposition) such as Winston Churchill and Ernest Shackleton come to mind.

It is a sign of one who will attempt the seemingly impossible. Often the aim is the good of mankind, frequently through scientific research ; sometimes it is less elevated and it has possibilities of violence. But always it appears to indicate one of exceptional powers.

The following examples may be recorded : Abbas Effendi, William Blake, S. T. Coleridge, Rupert Brooke, George Crabbe, George Elliot, Mrs. Eddy, President Ebert, Henry Ford, Pierpont Morgan, Mary Queen of Scots, Von Tirpitz, and Frederick the Great.

Something of the heroic temper of this opposition is shown in the case of Edith Allonby (N.N. 298) who committed suicide in order to draw attention, as she hoped, to the ideas contained in her book.

It would seem that both the last mentioned types are in some sense fighters, even if it be mental strife only, to use Blake's phrase.

(c) Sagittarius-Gemini seems to carry on the same propensities but more especially upon the mental plane. It is the disputant and arguer *par excellence*, particularly upon religious and philosophical problems. But it appears to produce fewer eminent men than the two preceding classes ; at all events, I find it harder to discover good examples. The common signs tend to a middle position in all respects ; they do not furnish either the heroes or the villains of the piece. Their chief activity is through thought, expressed vocally or by pen. While their thoughts may be astonishing, their actions are usually decorous and conventional.

This opposition may be expected to produce, other things being equal, intellectual restlessness, and possibly brilliance.   There may be pessimism (Thomas Hardy : Sun-Gemini opposition Saturn-Sagittarius) due to the failure to reconcile the aspirations of fire with the factual experience of air.

Sometimes this polarity produces the condition known as infantility, or the Peter Pan attitude towards life ; the refusal to leave the happy irresponsibilities of childhood and to grow up and accept the burdens of adult life. The native prefers the company of children to that of persons of his own age. There is a tendency to harp upon school-days and the " old school tie."

(6) Lastly, we have the three Earth-Water oppositions. These are the complementary opposites of the Fire-Air type and represent a tension in the two negative elements, which are nevertheless naturally akin and are essentially too sluggish to give rise to acute discords.

It is a matter of the struggle between the moods that arise, in the main, from sense-contacts and the compulsive pressures of the external world and its necessities. To take an all-too common experience in the lives of most of us, a man leaving a warm and comfortable bed on a frosty morning in order to eat his breakfast and catch his train—this might serve as a symbol of the kind of tension we have in mind. Something very everyday and by no means glorious.

It seems clear why we need not expect a sharp conflict here. For if the mind is satisfied to take things as it finds them, it is quite likely to acquiesce in the Epicurean view of life that will also satisfy the moods and senses.   It has indeed been said that " water and earth make mud," and certainly the less pleasant examples of this polarity can wallow in sensual enjoyment. It is indeed, a position that threatens too much liking for physical self-indulgence. One may instance George IV as a lazy, selfish sensualist (Moon conjunction Jupiter in Taurus, opposed to Mars).

At best it is an uninspiring formation, as pedestrian as Fire-Air is aetherial ; the essence of the downward-tending propensity.

Thus we have quoted Nietzsche under Fire-Air. But he had also Mars opposed to Jupiter, Virgo to Pisces, and here we see the " blond beast " element in his conceptions, which would have disgusted Annie Besant.

Even in its best manifestations the life-work will be found to be to some extent based upon the *physical*. Thus it occurs in nurses' and doctors' nativities. We find it in the natus of Dr. C. E. M. Joad (born 12 August, 1891) who has never shirked confessing to an enjoyment of the corporeal aspects of life.

(*a*) Taurus-Scorpio certainly points to an enjoyment of the things of the senses, possibly beyond the limits of dietetic discretion, and there is an obvious danger of precipitation in the form of disease, especially those forms which are of an auto-toxic nature. It is well known that George IV paid the price of his love of the table with gout and extreme obesity. In such a connection one must carefully study Mars and Saturn, to see how far physical activity and self-control are likely to counteract the voluptuous proclivities of the polarity. It is a rather dangerous combination, but to the native rather than to others.

(*b*) Virgo-Pisces has as an outstanding example (in terms of the Lights and also the two benefics) J. W. Goethe. It is an artistic and colourful polarity and has also a propensity for natural (and to some extent cryptic) science. It has also a sensuous aspect. As regards its occult leanings one may quote not only

Goethe but also Steiner, in whose nativity it also occurs twice (Sun-Saturn and Mercury-Neptune).

(*c*) Cancer-Capricorn is probably the most active and ambitious of the three types of this class of opposition. It has a flair for publicity and is often politically-minded. As Libra likes approval, so this polarity loves applause—the applause of crowds.

It is a sensitive and rather egocentric polarity.

At the present time it has a special interest for us because so many people now in early middle age were born when the Neptune-Uranus opposition in these signs was within orbs. It seems to have had its main precipitation (in this country and on the European continent) in the breaking up of innumerable homes during the war. Further, there has been a plethora of discussion on child-welfare and above all on the importance of the attitude of parents and of the home-environment generally in regard to the development of children. It may be well to stress this point of view, but astrologers know that the ability of even the wisest parents to produce good children by careful training is very limited. Marcus Aurelius is not the only good father to beget a Commodus.

To revert, this combination should in general be good at business and take a lively interest in politics. There should be considerable shrewdness and a tendency towards cynicism if Capricorn predominates, as against a credulous proclivity if Cancer is the stronger. This last appeared in three cases in which the Lights occupied these signs : Isaac Newton, W. T. Stead, and A. P. Sinnett.

Thus we conclude our studies of the square and opposition formations in terms of the signs.

When we turn to the harmonious, or, as we have suggested that they should be called, the facilitative aspects, we find that there are twelve possible trines, each sign throwing a trine to the next sign in the same element, and similarly there are twelve sextiles. To each of these a distinctive value belongs, and it will be our task to attempt a description, even if only a brief one, of each of them. We have said enough already about the basic significances of the Elements to make an a priori description easy ; but it is desirable to obtain, if possible, at least a few examples as checks upon our deductions and as illustrations.

Certain special formations deserve a few words.

The Grand Trine has come down to us with a bad name from the ancient astrologers. It is clear that it may denote a lack of balance, especially if more than three bodies are comprised in it. And lack of balance, in our estimation, is the worst of features.

But it seems also to tend towards a seeking of the easy way, avoidance of difficulties and dependence on others. It is an appeaser. Certainly it does not often appear in the nativities of " strong " men. Those who do reach important positions by reason of, or in spite of, this formation will usually be found to have been promoted by circumstance rather than by great merit.

The grand trine in Fire is naturally less dependent than the other three, but even so a peculiar involvement with others will often appear. It lacks strong individuality ; in politics it is a good party man.

It occurred in the natus of Neville Chamberlain, whose policy at the time of Munich led to the common use, in political jargon, of the term " appeasement."

Exceptions may be brought forward, as always in our science, but the above seems substantially true.

Other formations are the " Fan " type, when three bodies or groups of bodies are equidistant, e.g., a trine with another body in sextile to each, or a sextile with another planet in semisextile to each. There seems no reason why this term should not also apply to a square with another body in semisquare to each, though some might consider that in this case *flail* would be better than fan. The Grand Square, or Crucifix, and the " T " square (an opposition, with another body in square to each element) are familiar and unpopular groupings which usually generate or indicate, more power than the human frame can easily support. The Prince Consort's natus was an example of the Grand Cross, involving in his case the ruler and the four " malefic " planets. He was placed in a difficult and invidious position and was the victim of much misunderstanding and wilful attacks. His health was never robust and he died in early middle age.

Trines

(1) Aries to Leo.—A fine aspect for personal creative work. A good case is that of Alan Leo ; note how his personality played a large part in what he accomplished.

(2) Leo to Sagittarius.—A colourful character and a good deal of love of power, proud and " touchy " on personal matters.
    Disraeli (☽—☉) ; Robespierre (♂-♃).

(3) Sagittarius to Aries.—The power-seeking trait seems to appear also, with plenty of vigour, daring and independence.
    Queen Victoria (—♀), Nurse Cavell (♂ ☉-♅),
    Northcliffe (♃ — ☽), Bismarck (—☉).

We may note that strong Fire harmonies tend to produce what is called *personality* rather than great intellect, skill, knowledge or industry. Alan Leo, for example, was not a particularly learned or original astrologer, but, by his organising abilities and powers of leadership, he called forth brilliant work from others and laid down the path along which many followed in his footsteps.

(4) Taurus to Virgo.—A careful, conscientious craftsman or clerk. Examples amongst well-known* people appear to be rare.

(5) Virgo to Capricorn.—A good position for a student of science or politics. H. G. Wells is a case in point. ($\heartsuit$ $\odot$—$\mathcal{U}$).

(6) Capricorn to Taurus.—Another political combination, the Capricorn element seeming to dominate that of Taurus.

Hitler ($\mathcal{D}$ $\mathcal{U}$—$\odot$), W. Lilly ($\mathcal{D}$—$\odot$), Milton ($\hbar$—$\mathcal{D}$). Pasteur ($\odot$ etc. to $\hbar$) and Alfred R. Wallace (Ψ $\mathord{\text{H}}$—$\hbar$) represent natural science, often attractive to Earth signs.

It will be observed that the Earth-trine natives tend to be personally undistinguished, other things being equal, They are nearly all industrious—*workers* with mind or body. Care, patience and skill in action are their assets. Here lies their appropriate field for self-expression. If they are listened to with respect, it is not because of their personal attributes, but because of their practical skill and knowledge. When they desert their quiet unassuming rôle, they commonly make fools of themselves.

When we come to the Airy Trigon, we meet with the names of persons eminent in arts or letters ; we find the *thinkers*. They are usually less ordinary in appearance than the Earth-men, and may have grace and charm on the platform, but they sway by thought, not by " personal magnetism." They are concerned with more abstract subjects than the Earth-people, or at any rate their approach is more abstract and theoretical. Libra does introduce a certain element of personal attractiveness but it moves gently ; it is never the fervid orator, like Aries. It seeks to persuade, not overbear.

*The fact that examples have to be taken from collections of persons whose careers, for good or ill, were celebrated must be borne in mind. Otherwise wrong conclusions may be drawn.

(7) Gemini-Libra.—Here science is represented by Sir Humphrey Davy (♅—♂), letters by Erasmus (♃ — ☿), the films by Mary Pickford (♂ ♅—♄) and painting by David Wilkie (☽—♀).

(8) Libra-Aquarius.—Here we should expect letters and science to be to the fore. One would expect powers of lucid exposition. A lecturer on literature or science would be an appropriate métier.

Examples will easily be found.

(9) Aquarius-Gemini.—Cases are Maurice Hewlett, Thomas Hardy and Nell Gwyn—note the " common touch," so characteristic of Aquarius, in the two last.

Air is strongly associative and the trines in that Element are all extremely helpful in social life. On the other hand Water tends to shyness and a secluded life. There is a strong leaning towards arcane matters, probing the " secrets of nature," and so forth.

(10) Cancer-Scorpio.—Here we get John Dee (☉—♂) the picturesque Elizabethan alchemist, mathematician and astrologer, with his spiritualistic experiments and futile hunt for the secret of transmutation.

Another example is Thomas Hardy, who illustrates the melancholic and sordid side of this Element.

(11) Scorpio-Pisces.—This is probably the most courageous of the Water-combinations and is a good trine for a sea-faring career. It has a good example in R. L. Stevenson (☿ —♆ ☽)—courage in adversity, sea-stories, and the allegorical " Jekyll and Hyde "—note the effect of the double sign here. " Sepharial " is another case (♃ —☉).

(12) Pisces-Cancer.—A sympathetic motherly trine, with a strong tendency to the occult or metaphysical. Exx. are Baden Powell, Coue, Richard Garnett, A. P. Sinnett, and A. J. Balfour. It would also be a good business combination and occurs in the natus of J. D. Rockefeller (♅—☉).

We now come to the Sextiles, all of which have an affinity with the 3rd and 11th houses.

Those in Fire-Air often produce fine intellectual gifts with strong imaginative powers ; there is a certain element of inspiration here. Those in Earth-Water are matter-of-fact and businesslike, clever in practical things and averse to speculative thought.

(1) Aries-Gemini is a practical, sharp-witted, quick-thinking combination.

(2) Aries-Aquarius is more scientific and cultural, but is still mentally adventurous and self-reliant.

(3) Taurus-Cancer is probably an ideal business man's sextile shrewd, careful and with a sense of the public demand. It is also domestic and kindly. It is one of the most practical of positions. As an example, Cromwell (☉ ♉ ✶ ♃ ♋).

(4) Taurus-Pisces should also be good for business, but it is more idealistic than the foregoing and wider in its interests.

(5) Gemini-Leo would agree well with a writer for children, and in point of fact J. M. Barrie had it (♅— ☉) as well as such famous writers as Shaw (☽— ☉), Chesterton (☉—♅) and Tennyson (☽— ☉), so that it seems justifiable to claim that this is pre-eminently a writer's aspect, especially in the case of those who enjoy writing and do not write merely as a means of making money or to propagate some cause or theory.

(6) Cancer-Virgo is a shrewd and even cunning pair. It occurs in the nativities of Richelieu and Mussolini, but in

ordinary life it suggests abilities in commerce or domestic life.

(7) Leo-Libra is an essentially poetic and beauty-loving combination and is appropriate for any occupation that is concerned with ornament and decoration.

(8) Virgo-Scorpio is a good pair for a soldier or physician ; it is somewhat austere and reserved and finds no difficulty in being " cruel to be kind " ; it is capable of careful study and preparation and drastic action at the right moment, e.g., F. M. Montgomery (♂—♃ ☉ ☿). It is industrious, with plenty of care for detail, and critical (Sainte Beuve).

(9) Libra-Sagittarius harks back to the artistic or religious line of expression of Leo-Libra. It is usually clever and there are possibilities of brilliance here, but for ordinary pursuits it may be too idealistic and careless of material values.

(10) Scorpio-Capricorn would seem to be the ideal basis for a diplomatist or courtier, for there would be plenty of ability to use speech to dissemble thought, and probably also a liking for details of court-demeanour. Edward VII represents this type well and it is said he loved his rôle of kingship and also was punctilious over matters of court-ritual, military uniforms, and similar trivialities. Goethe spent much time on court functions and ceremonial and he has this pair represented not indeed by aspect, but by Saturn rising in Scorpio and the ruler Mars in Capricorn.

Goering's nativity has Sun in Capricorn and Moon in Scorpio and Goebbels' has the Lights in the same signs, but transposed. Note the former's love of uniforms and decorations.

(11) Capricorn-Pisces both have often a keen interest in natural history and scientific investigation, and so it is that we find Einstein has Sun in Pisces sextile Mars in

Capricorn, and similarly Isaac Newton had Sun in Capricorn forming a fan with bodies in Scorpio and in Pisces.

(12) Sagittarius-Aquarius produces two notable examples—Charles Dickens and Lewis Carroll. Of itself one would expect a rather satirical view of human nature from these two signs. It is interesting (though somewhat beside our main interests here) to note how the Sagittarius relationship with travelling appears in " Alice " and in several of Dickens' works, e.g., *Pickwick Papers*. It is exactly the sort of sign-duality from which clever skits and sketches on human nature might be expected.

Thus far with the Sextiles.

We now come to the last two whole-sign or multiples of 30° aspects, the semisextile or duodecile of 30° and the quincunx or inconjunct of 150°.

These necessarily involve a conflict of positive-negative polarity except in the rare cases of aspects of these orders that fall out of signs—rare, because of the narrowness of the orbs allowable. To express a purely personal opinion, the author considers the 30° contact to be almost negligible unless it is implicated in a larger formation, as for example Hitler's Sun 30° Neptune with two important planets midway between them. Nor is the writer prepared to agree with the usual a priori belief that it is an harmonious aspect. It has a 2nd house and 12th house relationship and sometimes the second of these is quite easily perceived, as indeed in Hitler's case, also *Notable Nativities* No. 653, " Scandals and Imprisonments."

The 150° contact is probably stronger. It is often important directionally, as bodies in radical square, trine or opposition pass to it. It has a 6th house and 8th house meaning and so often indicates deaths or illness.

It we are right in allowing only 1° of orb for these two classes of aspect, then they are naturally somewhat rare (except by direction).

We are now left with the 15° aspects, which I have named frictional, to indicate what is conceived to be their principal quality, namely, that they point to continual annoyance rather than definite and important events. One must mention here, however, the question of aspects that fall " out of signs." This condition arises with all aspects. A trine may always fall from the end of one sign to the beginning of the next, so that, though well within orbs, it does not lie within signs of the same Element.

Such cases really each require special consideration ; we can only say here that they are often held to be less strong than the aspects with normal emplacement, and this view is probably not ill-founded, for the harmony of the signs would correct at least to some extent the disharmony of the aspect, and conversely when the aspect is " good " and the signs mutually uncongenial.

When we come to the semisquare, sesquiquadrate and other 15° contacts—if others there be, as we believe is the case—then we find they really fall into two classes, on the average equally numerous. For anybody in the first half of (say) Aries and in sesquiquadrate to another in Leo will fall entirely in Fire and to that extent be harmonised, whilst anybody in the second half of Aries would throw its sesquiquadrate into Virgo, and suffer the reverse condition. Similarly the semisquare from the first half of Aries would fall in Taurus, but those from the second half would fall in the much more congenial Air-sign of Gemini.

It seems probable that 15° aspects falling in congenial signs may actually be facilitative rather than difficult ; at any rate it is reasonable to believe that they are better than the same contacts in uncongenial signs.

Indeed the whole thesis of this Chapter is to try to demonstrate how important sign-harmony is and how much can be judged from this alone, whereas hitherto nearly all the emphasis has commonly been laid on the bodies forming the aspect, the signs being given a quite secondary value. That their significance is secondary to that of the bodies may be true ; but they are far from unimportant.

It should be noted that the sign-combinations of which we have spoken may operate quite powerfully without aspects, if the two Elements are heavily tenanted, as by satellitia. An example, in terms of national psychology, is the commonly accepted map for the United States of America, wherein two planets rise in Gemini and the Sun and three planets are in Cancer. Here an Air-Water clash is quite apparent in the antithesis of the " hard-boiled " attitude that Americans sometimes display on the one hand and their evident emotionalism on the other. The Moon and Saturn are also in Air, and the latter does actually form a close square to the Sun, but even without any such contact a conflict would occur, though in more general terms than is the case when a near aspect provides a focus.

Morin, the famous French astrologer, had planets in Aquarius and Pisces, and so, too, had C. W. Leadbeater : this is in excellent agreement with writers who treated cryptic subjects in a scientific spirit—so far as this is possible. In the case of a Roman Catholic missionary, described as "full of candour, simplicity and devotion" and born at Tours, 5.00 a.m., 12 August, 1861, we find Sun and two planets rising in Leo and three more planets in Virgo : this agrees well with the life—love expressed in service.

Since the sequence of the signs is obviously not meaning-less, but quite otherwise, it is plain that a strong emphasis on two consecutive signs should have a potentially harmonious value. This condition ought to make for a definite career as distinct from the scattered composition of some horoscopes, which indicates a diffusion of interests. It is a sort of integration by concentration.

CHAPTER VI

THE FIRST SIX OR NORTHERN SIGNS

PERHAPS a few preliminary reflections on the subject of the zodiac itself would not be out of place.

The dictionary defines it for us simply enough as a belt in the heavens extending some 18° on either side of the ecliptic, which is the circle described by the apparent motion of the Sun arising from the earth's annual revolution around that body.

So far, so good.

But whilst there is but one zodiac there are of course an infinite number of ways in which it may be subdivided. Modern astrologers, in the west, commonly use but one : starting from the first point of Aries, which is the point at which the ecliptic intersects the equator and commences its northern arc, we divide the ecliptic into twelve exactly equal areas of 30° each.

How did this procedure first arise ?

There are, of course, twelve well-known zodiacal constellations, or star-groups, which bear the same names as the twelve signs. At some time, perhaps (to follow Maurice Wemyss' suggestion) about A.D. 548, these constellations coincided with the signs of the same name ; but, owing to the phenomenon of equinoctial precession, this is no more the case, and it is supposed that at the present time the first point of Aries had retrograded, in relation to the constellations, about 19°, so that it is about two-thirds of the way through the constellation Pisces and will in due course enter Aquarius.

It seems probable that the original zodiac was that of the twelve constellations, since the early observer is more likely to have noted groups of stars than to have formed

the theory of a zodiac of exactly equal dimensions beginning from the first point of Aries.

But when more exactitude was called for, the fact that
the twelve constellations were of irregular extent probably
bothered him ; and it would seem, he stumbled, by chance
or inspiration, upon the notion of a precise 30° division of
the zodiac, being ignorant, until the time of Hipparchus
(2nd century B.C.), that the precession of the equinoxes
would gradually force him to a decision as to which was
the true zodiac—that of the signs always commencing
from 0° Aries or of the constellations beginning with the
constellation of the Ram.   The Hindus have to this day
remained loyal to the constellations ; we, in the west,
have almost without exception cleaved to the zodiac of
the signs.

The school of thought that tends to regard astrology as a
" natural " science will probably find it difficult to suppose
that the zodiac is really the mathematically perfect creation
that the twelve equal signs present to us, whereas those
who adhere to a more Platonic—or perhaps we shoud say,
Pythagorean—point of view will find this an outstanding
example of the truth of their much-quoted dictum that
" God geometrises."

Maurice Wemyss attributes validity to both zodiacs,
with a good deal of reason on his side, but in practice very
few western astrologers concern themselves, except very
fitfully, with the constellations.   It is obvious that to depart
from the sign-zodiac and adopt that of the stars would
involve declaring that all the astrology of the last few
centuries, or at any rate most of it, was rubbish and that
those who had thought otherwise were self-deluded.
No such step appears remotely necessary.

However, no one has the right to say that this 30°
division of the ecliptic alone is right and justified.   The
Chinese have another division altogether, and the Hindus

use the lunar mansions as another mode of division. If they consider that these methods are of proven value, we have no right to reject their views without examination. Nor have they the right to condemn ours.

Turning now to the individual signs, we have, in treating of the elements and quadruplicities, said much concerning them. As to whether it is possible for us to discover a basic meaning or value for each, opinions must differ. It would probably be safe to say that no one has succeeded in doing so. *They themselves* are basic words, reasons, or Logoi.

Alan Leo's works contain more than one attempt to apply one all-explanatory word to each sign. Isabelle Pagan has written with great charm and insight on them, and we owe much to W. H. Sampson's brilliant treatise. These are all valuable attempts to illuminate profound mysteries, but it is certain that none of these writers would claim for a moment to have reached an entirely satisfactory and, therefore, final result. Indeed, were a such complete solution of these enigmata to be attained, the framework of human knowledge would have been perfected and only a process of filling-in would remain to us.

But this is impossible. It is of the essence of a true mystery that it is for ever capable of yielding further illumination and can never be exhausted in its ultimate profundity. And, because the zodiacal mysteries embrace all manifested things, whether the manifestation is interior or exterior, subjective or objective, so it is true to say that all things end in mystery—*omnia abeunt in mysterium.*

If there be any scientific path by which man can intellectually approach the Supreme Mystery, which Plato denominated THE ONE AND THE GOOD, from below, then it seems that it must first traverse the

Zodiacal Mysteries, which contain all the secrets of the manifestation of That One in the lower worlds.

Here we shall attempt to throw some little light on the signs from the *individual psychological* angle, just as, in a previous work,* we have tried to do the same from a cosmic point of view. What is the ultimate meaning, so far as we can penetrate, of these Divine Signatures so far as the present-day living and struggling man or woman is concerned, and how are they likely to exhibit their values in his or her life ? That is the present problem. We have designated the subject as a mystery and we approach it in a spirit of humility, content if we can throw but a little further light upon it in some few minds and preferring to say too little rather than too much. It seems right, also, to seek to express an original line of thought rather than to serve the reader with long extracts from the works of others, however illuminating these may be, or, what is worse, to rewrite what others have stated without troubling to acknowledge the source of one's recitals.

Nor will we seek to write from any particular philosophical standpoint, for, painful though such a statement may be to the enthusiastic devotees of this or that school of thought, it is not they who hold the keys to the zodiacal temple, but it is in the principles of the zodiac that the explanation of their doctrines lie. Just as the reasons for the deficiencies and distortions that disfigure partitive teachings are to be found in the failure properly to understand these principles.

Therefore if we wish to approach the study of the zodiac under the most promising conditions, we must try to do so with open minds. Wishful thinking and mental preconceptions should be banished, so far as is humanly possible.

It is not for us to mould these mysteries to our liking. How absurd is the common talk of " ruling one's stars " !

*In Chapter III of *The Zodiac and the Soul.*

There are but two possible positions to consider : one can turn one's back on these matters in mere ignorance, or one can seek intelligently to co-operate with them. Even co-operation is a bold word to use ; obedience would be better.

Not that we would imply that co-operation with divine principles is impossible without a technical knowledge of astrology. One can, obviously, express the Spiritual Values, of which the signs are symbolical, without knowing them by astrological names, or by any names at all for that matter. But whether one can study them scientifically by any other system, except that Integral Teaching which embraces all approaches to truth, I do not know. Certainly the pathway would be much harder to tread. McDougall has tabulated his specific instincts as a result of studies from which presumably astrology was excluded ; but he reached the significant number twelve and many of them are right in the line of our thought. One can assert that had he spent two or three weeks in the study of such a book as that of W. H. Sampson, to which we have referred above, and had *then* co-ordinated his own conceptions with those of astrology, he would have reached a better conclusion in much less time.

Thus we regard the zodiac as furnishing an absolute criterion of truth so far as the manifest universe is concerned. Once win to a true conception of these principles, and one has a perfect yardstick to which all else must conform, or stand convicted of error.

In studying the signs in actual horoscopes it is best to use the Sun positions, rather than the ascendant, that is, if we desire to see the sign at its best. Doubtless there are exceptional cases, but as a general rule the signs appear to show their values to most advantage when the Sun is placed in them, and that is perhaps not strange, since they are divisions of the ecliptic, which is the solar path. Thus,

Sun in Aries usually has not the rudeness that often appears when Aries rises ; Sun in Taurus is firm, but Taurus rising is often obstinate and unreasonable, and so on.

ARIES

From the standpoint of individual psychology one might perhaps call the first four signs, comprising as they do one sign of each Element, as *experimental*. In them we seem to see the subject experimenting with fresh powers.

Aries is the Beginning.   It is the simple assertion *I Am*.   It does not make this affirmation in any metaphysical spirit.   It is far from the fields of metaphysical investigation and theorising.   It is the simple consciousness of existence, and, being Fire, it receives this fact intuitively and not by any pondering upon self and not-self.   Later on, transcendental philosophies may speak of the merging of the soul into the All, of losing the self to win the Self, of the sense of at-one-ness with all things.   Nothing is further from the Arietic instinct.   It is most certain that it is a distinct being, not only separate from all else, but not even linked to others at all closely by sympathy or affection. It dislikes all appearance of ties and even in its vocation seeks a job of its own.   It is neither specially creative nor destructive ; it *is*.   There is no impulse to create, for this would mean concerning oneself with something other than the self, and there is no need to destroy because that again means occupying oneself with the not-self, unless of course this interferes with the personal self-expression.

But Aries is indeed a grand fighter when some other element in the geniture does forge a link with the rest of the world.   Zola, for example, had a satellitium of great power in this sign.   But it was in close contact with Neptune in Aquarius, and *thence* came the link with the dregs of mankind, to say nothing of a close conjunction in

Pisces, also in contact with the Aries group. Of itself, Aries fights when *personally* vexed or impeded.

Its pugnacity also has another origin. As the sign of beginnings it likes new ideas and new movements, and this naturally enough leads to conflicts with the established form of things.

The faults and virtues of the sign are easily traced to its essential nature. It is impatient, for it has not had time to learn anything by experience and it has the natural vigour of the steed that has just started the race. It is unsympathetic, or at least indifferent, because its very nature compels it to be self-conscious (on the instinctive level of course) and not other-conscious. It is rash—but also brave—through lack of imagination. It is apt to be boastful of its own achievements, for that is where its interests lie. It shares with another fire-sign, Sagittarius, a tendency to exaggerate in order to achieve effect and call attention to what it is saying. It is generous—or at least free-handed—because it does not wish to be cluttered with possessions, for which it cares nothing. It is capable in a purely personal way but fails when it has to deal with complicated circumstances, which try its patience, and with other people, in whom it is not interested. Its intrinsic nature makes it self-reliant and its impulse is to be frank, honest and aboveboard, for it is too unsophisticated to dissemble. Besides, disguise is to hide the self, to proclaim which is the very message that Aries comes to deliver, in loud and unabashed egotism. Its financial probity is due to the same cause as its generosity with its possessions—it is not attached to things. It is like the good soldier who refuses to load himself with loot, not because he has any moral objection to looting but because he does not wish to be impeded by it.

In fact, just as we end the zodiacal journey in the disillusionment and spiritual non-attachment of Pisces, so we begin with the material non-attachment of Aries. Libra demands its due, that and no more ; Aries does not even bother to collect its patrimony but hastens to " go about its Father's business " whereunto it was sent into manifestation from the void. And the Father is symbolised by the Sun, exalted in Aries. Aries is the primary Incarnation of the Supernal Fire, a Child or Youth, with all the failings of adolescence, but with its promise also.

The contrast between two opposed signs is obvious, but there is always a sharp differentiation that almost amounts to opposition between a sign and the two others that flank it on either side. Pisces is the dust and ashes of the burntout fire, from which, we may trust, the Phoenix of resurrection has taken wing ; Aries is the new beginning.

Next we come to

TAURUS

Here we find many resemblances to Aries but a great difference. There is nothing of non-attachment in this sign. Here the ego has veritably discovered the wonders and delights of the external world, beginning with its own body.

Aries uses its physical vehicle as just that—a channel or instrument for its self-expression. If it falls sick, the response is impatience, and probably drastic remedies will be applied, but rest, unless this is forced upon it, it will not.

Taurus quickly discovers that the body may be an instrument of delight and self-indulgence. The self of Aries is not concerned to think about its bodily likes and dislikes, but Taurus emphatically is. It looks upon the whole of Nature, including the body, as a feast to be enjoyed. It is not a mere field for action, an arena wherein to display one's prowess, to Taurus, a fixed and, therefore, pleasure-pain conscious sign, as it is to Aries the cardinal.

Nor does Taurus wish to alter anything, for normally all is much to its taste. Mind has not yet arrived to inquire into whys and wherefores and speculate as to possible improvements. Taurus browses bull-like in the pastures of the world. Its wants are simple and basic—sex, shelter and food.

Thus it sets to work to rear a family, to build and to plough. Further anxieties and exertions are a waste of time and a vexation. The affirmation of the sign is *I possess and I enjoy*. In other words, there is a world around me some of which is pleasant, and this I propose to appropriate and call mine. Yet it is not precisely acquisitive in an active sense. The Taurean procedure is not so much to " get up and get " as to sit down upon something and assert that henceforth it is to be his. He is the true originator of the " squatter's title " of our law. Nutrition is probably the correct allocation here from McDougall's list.

He is, however, notably honest, because all fixed signs tend to have a respect for law and order, as being themselves of a fixed character, and because his wants are simple and because quarrelling in any case is a disturbing thing. However, he is far more concerned about his possessions than is Aries, and when he falls into crime, it is usually because his property has been encroached upon, just as Aries resents infringements of his liberty of action. But Aries, in his youthful self-expressions, often treads on other people's toes in sheer unawareness of there being such things ; Taurus has become aware of others without being interested in them or troubling to understand them ; however, he can perceive that they probably resemble himself in their outlook and is prepared to respect their rights of ownership.

He contrasts with Aries mainly in two points : he is contented instead of discontented, and he is patient instead of being the reverse. Both these virtues arise chiefly from fixity ; if one desires things to remain as they are, then it is not difficult to be satisfied because, after all, things usually *do* remain as they are, at least in the countryside where the typical Taurus native resides, or in the old-established businesses that attract him if he is a city-dweller. If an attempt is made to force change upon him, he is usually anything but contented or patient, but on the contrary he reacts violently and displays his primitive instincts quite as clearly as does Aries.

He is also much more of a disciplinarian than Aries, again because of the awareness of other people who may interfere with his routine. To discipline others requires time and patience, and long before the child has been moulded as Aries would wish, this sign has lost interest in the task of character-formation.

These two signs are definitely the two primitive *par excellence* and a heavy emphasis on both in the same natus presents a difficult problem.

All fixed signs have a power-seeking propensity. Some may call this a complex but it is the reverse of complex ; it is extremely simple and arises quite naturally from the idea of fixation. Each fixed sign, in some sense, wants to retain things as they are, provided of course they are as he wishes. Now it is only by the exercise of power that man can produce a condition that he likes and then hold it, or try to hold it, in perpetuity without change. Each fixed sign sees power as attractive for some distinct reason, though it is probable that power in itself has a natural appeal to every man. For Taurus it ministers to bodily enjoyment in food, sex and home and there is for them a sensuous joy in beholding their own parklands and cornfields.

Now in contrast to Taurus we find in Scorpio a deep dissatisfaction, and in place of easy contentment with things as they seem there is a profound urge to analyse and examine. The table which Taurus found good to eat upon is found by Scorpio to be composed of electric charges and, if it is, Taurus would reply, in the improbable case of his having read the classics,

" Cur quis non prandeat, hoc est ? "
" Is that a reason for missing lunch ? "

GEMINI

Taurus having experimented with gross matter and pronounced it very good, the next sign experiments with mind, also with gusto. Here we have McDougall's Curiosity. The affirmation of Gemini might be *I am Interested*. " Interesse " =to be between or among.

Its interests are endless but somewhat superficial, for, though man has now discovered his mind and the intelligibility of things, we are still in the Elemental Tetrad, to use W. H. Sampson's adjective, and it is still an essentially child-mind. There is, for example, no appreciation of truth as such ; only a revelation that things are intelligible and that there is an infinite delight in understanding them. It is, perhaps, essentially on a level with the child's pleasure in taking things to pieces to " see how they work." Indeed, in a primitive specimen of the sign, it is almost a simian curiosity ; or the " satiable curiosity" of Kipling's baby-elephant. It learns easily but it easily forgets, for the motive is still that of pleasure ; there is no sense of duty.

Nor is the moral sense yet developed. Morality arises in our relations with others, and, though Gemini as an air-sign has its associative propensity and actually rules one's near relatives (according to tradition) yet it is still highly self-centred and is perhaps on an average as selfish as its two zodiacal predecessors. Its mental activities therefore are amoral, and it is well known that an affliction in Mercurial signs tends to acquisitive dishonesty, Gemini thus becoming the not unwilling agent of the Taurean desire for possession.

The mutable factor introduces flexibility and a power of adaptation that is exactly the reverse of the Taurean stability. But the mind is equally concerned with the objective world. Here is the broad difference between Gemini and its zodiacal opposite ; it is not philosophical or concerned with abstract reasons. It likes to collect facts. It is mind directed towards utilisation, or just mind enjoying the experience of using its own faculties. In matters beyond its own scope it is often agnostic or even flippant.

It is the first sign with a human symbol and appropriately the Twins are children.

And because Gemini is human, though childlike, it cannot repose as does Taurus in the bosom of Mother Nature or consent to a merely natural evolutionary progress. Hence, under Gemini, we get education. It is the sign of the school and scholar.

Furthermore it is mutable and the fact that each fixed sign is followed by a mutable indicates the reawakening of the spirit of unrest and agitation that must come to prevent stagnation. In Gemini we have the principle of inter-communication, by all means—travel, letters, speech, telephone and telegraph.

It is the sign of the constantly questioning child that does not always wait for an answer, that on being told that a certain animal is a cow, asks " Why ? "

Thus, indeed, the Mercurial gadfly stings Taurus and drives it unwillingly, as in the Io myth, over land and sea.

So it is that the combination, by planetary emphasis, of Taurus and Gemini is not, in the writer's experience, a very happy one. " Mens agitat molem." Mother Nature has borne a strange and mischievous child with new-fangled ideas, one might say. It is from the Taurean point of view, very sad and puzzling. Taurus, in a certain sense. represents a primitive Paradise, though not the idealised Paradise or Elysium of Libra. These signs are related by quincunx, and so also Scorpio, the tempter, has a quincunx relation with Gemini, which, if not a tempter, is at least a disturber.

In a previous work the writer has related Gemini with the principle of distinctiveness, or the fact of difference. Thus Gemini perceives these differences and yet, as an air sign, is associative. And here is no contradiction, because there would be no reason to associate things which are mere duplicates ot each other. But Gemini can only bring things into contact with one another ; it leaves the work of unification to Libra. It is connective but not unitive.

CANCER

To those who are chiefly developed on the mental side, as is so often the case in the modern world, the passage from Gemini to Cancer seems a retrogression. After attaining the keen if limited mentality of Gemini, what a fall it seems to pass back to a sign that is largely instinctive and has the reputation of wallowing in emotion, especially of the gloomier kind ! Moreover, Cancer is the sign of the family, household or clan, and it is often marked with distinct limitations, even on the emotional level ; it is subject to all sorts of prejudices as soon as the clan interests are involved. This is nowhere more in evidence than amongst the Scotch, a Cancer nation ; and in China, too, there is one moral code governing one's dealings with those within the clan and another for those who are without.

The distinction between the frankly corporeal enjoyments of Taurus and the imaginative joys and sorrows of Cancer is very plain. For instance, in love it is the physical contact that appeals to the former sign, but for Cancer it is the emotional and fantasy-formed elements that provide the pleasure.

At its lower level one sees Cancer well illustrated by a women's tea-meeting, whereat the principal items of conversation are disease and operations, intimately described, and interminable family gossip.

Why does all this primitivity succeed the clear light of Gemini, wherein men are beginning to be truly human, real thinkers ?

It must be admitted that, if all the signs are true mysteries, the water trigon presents the three most abstruse arcana of the zodiac. Nor are they of a cheerful character. One has only to consider the rulerships of the three corresponding houses : the Grave, Death and Imprisonment.

In a sense all three signs of this triplicity are connected with *dissolution*, with some form of death. They are potentially tragic, all waters of the Red Sea through which one can pass only by an act of faith ; and they all follow what seems to be a great achievement. In the case of Cancer, after the discovery of mind.

Gemini is a bright and happy sign ; Cancer a fearful one. We may say that its affirmation is : *I feel and I fear*. Feeling is an ambiguous word. We do not mean, of course, the bodily feelings of Taurus, but those of the emotional nature.

Cancer is Mother Nature. Not physical nature, which is shown in the earthy trigon, but the formative forces behind it. And Nature is a timid mother, in one aspect she is Niobe weeping for her slain children, killed because she exulted in them too much. She is protective, and one cannot be usefully protective unless one is for ever on the alert against danger, never asleep at one's post.

The attachment to tribe and family and children is due to the instinct for self-protection. It is the first sign of that gregarious tendency which comes to flower in Aquarius. By loyalty to larger groups one earns the protection of these agglomerates. Amongst them one is happy and at home ; beyond their pale one is shy, distressed and perhaps even afraid. A Saturn-Cancer contact often produces this condition in a marked degree, even to the extent of phobia, a pressure of the irrational upon the rational nature.

On the other hand, Cancer is cardinal, and despite its sensitiveness this part of its nature often forces it into the limelight, and, once having overcome its shyness, it seems to have no objection to this illumination. In this the shyness of Cancer differs from that of Virgo, a sign which is often content to be a recluse and avoid society.

Despite their divergences, the combination of Gemini and Cancer in one map, by planetary stress, is not always a misfortune. It makes a good imaginative writer, e.g., Sir Rider Haggard (Sun and Saturn rising in Cancer, two planets in Gemini) or Thomas Hardy (Sun and two planets in Gemini, Moon in Cancer). Note, in both cases, interest in the land.

Of all planets it is probable that Venus is strongest in Cancer and is better than the Moon itself in this sign, since this may overemphasise the lunar power. Just as, on the other hand, the Moon is traditionally strong in Taurus, where its anxieties are lulled to rest.

The opposition of Cancer to Capricorn represents the antagonism between natural and artificially organised social groupings. Cancer grouping depends on blood and race ; Capricorn upon political expediencies. And we see this opposition in the Nazi state, not at all unexpectedly, since this opposition occurs powerfully in the German " Versailles " horoscope. Ostensibly preaching the natural ties of race and blood, the Nazis were quite prepared to develop on the lines of " scientifically " organised breeding and to confer " honorary " Teutonism upon strangers who served their purpose.

But all oppositions are potentially beneficial if the antithesis can be synthesised. Cancer needs the restraints of the Goat and this in turn can derive much help from the sure instinctive insight of the Crab.

It is probable that several of McDougall's instincts have a lunar kinship, i.e., nutrition, flight and, most of all, acquisition. Cancer is the collector ; it has the squirrel tendency to lay up for future use, a useful propensity undoubtedly for a sign that precedes the profusion of Leo. It is part of the general Cancer impulse to fortify its position, to " mak siccar " in the language of a Cancer nation.

This collecting proclivity extends to many things, from land and houses to postage stamps and candle ends.

Other natural devices for self-protection which are of a Cancer character are the thick hide of the rhinoceros, the plated armour of the armadillo, the holes and burrows of certain animals, the camouflage of the chameleon and hundreds of other species from moth to zebra, and the tenacious hold of the limpet amid the surging tides.

The last is an illuminating example ; Cancer is always the limpet seeking the rock upon which it can take firm hold amid the swirl of change.

LEO

The second fire-sign of the zodiac brings a further influx of the divine creative energy.

Leo has not been always kindly treated by astrological

writers, perhaps because so many of these, naturally enough, are Mercurians, who, once again naturally, do not seem to appreciate the greatness of the sign. At all events, references have been made to the opinion, common among zoologists, that the lion is not as brave an animal as he looks, as well as to the fact that Leo shares with Scorpio the distinction of being one of the two unpleasant, and in fact dangerous, zodiacal animals. He is indeed the only predatory one so far as the human point of view goes. However, mankind has always used the lion as a symbol of grandeur and kingship.

Leo is the creative sign *par excellence*. Cancer, as the Mother, must share this distinction ; but it is Leo which corresponds to the 5th house, the house of offspring.

But Leo is much more than merely philoprogenitive. It is a sign of creative art, particularly those forms of art that are directly concerned with the expression of beauty rather than truth. Leo is not a writer ; it writes badly, even clumsily and carelessly. It is not a particularly fluent speaker. But in the cultured Leo there is a deep sense of beauty and love of it.

It is true that, in the world of affairs, Leo often seems to reach positions rather by some innate power of its own than by anything that it has actually done. It can inspire and vitalise others, who have better brains but less vision and faith. This was eminently the case with Alan Leo. In any sphere of life it was no mean thing for a man with only an elementary education (in both senses) to write books that have been translated into several foreign languages. He has been accused of having got others to do much of the writing for him ; but, after all, he got the books written ; they would not have come into existence without him. He revivified astrology ; he made many intelligent and educated men see that it was *worth while*. Under his guidance the dead bones came to life ; and of the many thousands who now study the subject in the English-speaking countries, how many must owe their introduction to it, however indirectly, to him ?

We do not write this merely as a digressive enconium upon our old and honoured leader ; but because it would seem to be true, *mutatis mutandis*, of many sons of the sign and their work.

Others have had greater technical knowledge, have written with greater insight and a much wider range of general culture and literary finish, but how many will be respected as men to the extent that he deserves to be ?

Thus, as with all fixed signs, it seems that it was what Leo *is* rather than what he *does* that matters.

Nevertheless there is a real goodness in the true Leo, a warm kindness of heart and unselfish affection that is rare in other signs. It helps readily, but not only materially, or even chiefly. Its very presence fortifies and cheers.

It is the sign of the Divine Splendour.

Yet, it is symbolised by an animal, and in this sign man is not beyond the dangers of a relapse to the natural kingdom and the irrational passions.

True magnanimity is the right self-expression of the native of Leo, the ability to see all things largely and completely.

The failing is pride, not the sensitive pride of Scorpio, but rather pride that is of the nature of vanity. There is the temptation to say " For *mine* is the kingdom, the power and the glory," to which the bombastic Italian dictator, with Sun and Mercury conjoined in this sign, so completely succumbed. Hence your weak Leo is easily flattered and even befooled. There is often a hunger for affection and a proneness to deep hurt if this is not forthcoming in the abundant measure that Leo gives and longs to receive. It is notoriously liable to be unfortunate in marriage, probably for this reason.

It seems likely that the Founder of the Christian religion was born under Leo, or perhaps with the Sun in that sign.* At least I cannot think of any other sign as being likely for this Incarnation. At any rate, His teaching as recorded in the Gospels is characterised by many features that are purely Leonine. In particular this is true of the emphasis laid on faith, for if the affirmation of Cancer is I fear, that of Leo is *I Have Faith*. And this is as it should be, for as the Sun is the power behind all life, so faith is the base of all our activities and no so-called rationalism can escape this fact. For even the rationalist has to assume the validity of reason ; reason cannot be used to demonstrate its own veracity ; and, if we make experience our criterion, we have to assume the reliability of memory.

It is true that in Christianity there are also strong Piscean traits, and, for that matter, Aquarian too. But the character of the Founder is largely Leonine ; the Piscean features belong rather to the idealised Jesus of the churches and perhaps have not helped to a true understanding of the Gospels.

Certainly the Geniture of the Incarnation may have had strong Pisces elements ; that would be quite likely. But it cannot be questioned that Jesus was a man of extraordinary power and authority, who impressed people greatly by his very presence ; and this strongly indicates Leo. Moreover the reiterated references to Sonship point to the same sign. Strangely, Leo is both the Sun and the Son, through its 5th-house relationship.

How Leonian are the opening and closing phrases of the Lord's Prayer !

Incidentally, the first petition is clearly that of Virgo, the Maiden with the sheaf of corn. The next passage, with

*That Jesus was born at Christmas is of course a solar-rebirth detail. The shepherds would not have been watching their sheep by night in the plains at that season.

its spirit of mutuality—" forgive us our trespasses as we
forgive them that trespass against us "—is Libra, just as
surely as the prayer to be delivered from evil is the entreaty
of Scorpio.

Thus the four central signs of the zodiac are unmistakably represented

Astrologers who wish to interpret religion according to
their science must regard the Sun as the symbol of Deity,
at least of this system, and for them, therefore, the
attributes of Leo are veritably divine. Indeed we can
study the nature of God in a scientific manner by examining the Sun in its highest aspects, not as a vain and self-
seeking magnate but as a source of tender affection and
loving fatherhood for all upon whom its rays may shine.

In this way astrology provides a *scientific* revelation of
the Divine Being.

Considering Leo in terms of its opposition to Aquarius,
we see here man as an individual contrasted with collective
mankind. Therefore our remarks on page 91 are easily
understood. When the opposition is reconciled, there is
the chance of a great leader of the many appearing. When
the opposition is in full play either the individual will
reject the collective, or vice versa. A case in point might
be Robespierre, with two malefics setting in opposition
(perhaps closer than the recorded time allows) to an
Aquarian ascendant. Compared with Leo, the Saturnian
sign is cool, aloof, and non-attached, though in certain
conditions it displays a more Uranian quality and is
violent and drastic. This agrees well enough with the
characteristics of the " people " at large ; they are
usually indifferent and difficult to interest in their own
welfare, but are liable to sudden outbreaks of anger.

Leo is the aristocrat—in its true light it is the *real*
aristocrat, not merely the scion of a long line. Aquarius is
the democrat. One could compile a long list of the dictators

of the 1930's and 1940's and find not a single planet in this sign.

Contrasting Leo with the two quincuncial signs, Capricorn and Pisces, we are struck, as one usually is in these comparisons, by the dissimilarities. Truly the quincunx is the inconjunct relationship, as the Americans frequently call it—the relationship which hardly exists. Again we may refer to the way in which the Leonine Jesus detested the Capricorn Pharisees and their ways. Some of those Pharisees, after all, must have been honest men, according to their lights ! They can hardly have *all* been hypocrites. But there is something in Capricorn that Leo cannot tolerate.

Leo and Pisces are not so hostile ; indeed, who can dislike Pisces ? But a strong Piscean element seems to bring out the worst side of Leo ; it weakens it, and a self-indulgent tendency will often be apparent.

The true self-expression of the Leo is in love, not the passionate or the sentimental varieties, but pure goodness of heart towards all. And, objectively, in leadership through character and the manifestation of the vitalising power.

Among McDougall's instincts it seems that both the reproductive and the parental might be placed under Leo.

VIRGO

Having left Leo, we come to the second sign of the Earth Trigon.

In Virgo the crude matter of Taurus becomes refined and we notice, at once, a more delicately organised corporature, to the welfare of which the native often devotes time and attention. It is the sign of physical culture, hygiene and remedial and preventive medicine.

In much the same way the instinctual delight in the

physical world which is apparent in Taurus becomes a careful study thereof in Virgo, a study which is not directed so much towards enjoyment as utilisation. Thus Virgo is the sign of the handicrafts and of horticulture and agriculture, particularly in their more scientific aspects.

It offers many points of contrast with Leo. It is not the sign of leadership but of service; it does not aim at brilliant results but at useful ones. It is patient and does not turn from routine and drudgery; it hates show and shuns responsibility and publicity. It is not ambitious but is satisfied with a straight job and a fair wage.

In some respects it is not a fortunate sign, from a worldly standpoint. It often suffers from shyness and lack of social ease and confidence. Sometimes the sense of inadequacy—the much-discussed inferiority complex—reacts in apparent conceit and also in a carping hyper-criticalness of others. Mars in Virgo can be rough, as was exemplified by the rude camp-life manners of Napoleon I ; Saturn in Virgo is often depressed and depressing. Even Venus and Jupiter lose their true graces in this sign ; there is a lack of expansiveness.

Do we know the true ruler of this sign ? Of all the ancient Pantheon it is perhaps most reminiscent of Vulcan, the lame smith whose gaucherie evokes the laughter of the gods. Lameness and deafness are associated with Virgo.

But as the name of the sign is that of the Maiden we must find an appropriate ascription amongst the virgin-goddesses of the classic world. Pallas Athene naturally comes to mind ; she was the patroness of the arts and sciences and the Romans used the word Minerva—her Latin cognate—to mean mother-wit or good sense. But Pallas was also a warrior-goddess and that seems quite inappropriate to the mild and inoffensive Virginian.

Nor can we connect him with Diana. We come quite easily to Proserpine or Persephone, the daughter of Ceres, about whom there is told the familiar tale of her being ravished away from earth by Pluto and forced to spend half the year in the underworld as queen of the dead. This obviously refers, at least in its exoteric aspect, to the death of vegetation in winter and its renewal in the spring, and it is quite in accord with the known relationship of the sign to green nature.

As the bride of Dis or Pluto we might expect that Virgo would be opposed to Scorpio, as the death-sign. But Pisces, as we shall see, is also a sign of physical dissolution. There is certainly a clear opposal between the neat and precise Virgo, with its keen sense of fact and actuality, and the diffuse and careless Pisces with its dreams and visions. Whilst the emotions of the Fishes flow in all directions, Virgo is self-controlled and limited in its sympathies, with a strong belief that charity begins at home ; indeed it is usually a self-centred sign, closing as it does the first or limited half of the zodiac, after which each sign tends to present the principles of its opposite in an expanded form. Thus Virgo serves its master faithfully, he being the individualised man, Leo. Pisces serves humanity— Aquarius.

We have already noted that there is often a strange link between signs in quincunx relationship. Venus and Mars, for example, rule signs in this affinity. Virgo and Aquarius are the Maid and the Man (mankind would be better, but the symbol is a man). The only other fully human symbol is that of the Twins. If we follow W. H. Sampson in naming Aquarius the sign of Civilisation, then Virgo, as craftsman, lies at the base of *our* civilisation and it is in fact a truly civilised sign. In fact, to most people civilisation *is* craftsmanship. It is often jokingly said of the Americans, the most highly civilised of nations *in this sense,* that they judge civilisation by the local standard of plumbing.

Daedalus, the Greek prototype of all inventors, seems a Virginian figure, and the myth of his flight from Crete with his son Icarus, who soared too high and lost his wings under rays of the sun, seems to refer to the ambitions of Capricorn, the 5th sign from Virgo. The story of his making a wooden cow for Pasiphaë may point to the possible reversion of Virgo to the animal conditions of Taurus.

Virgo, Libra and Scorpio surely represent the Garden of Eden, Adam and Eve, and the Serpent, respectively. Perhaps the centaur Sagittarius stands for the alternatives : further growth in the company of the Gods or reversion to a subhuman state.

It is clear that Mercury, the power of intelligence, will be subjected, in its earthy aspect in Virgo, to the temptation to use its capabilities in a merely pragmatic field and to neglect ideal considerations. Man, in Virgo, acquires actual power over natural existences and forces, as distinct from power in potential, in Leo. He has to make the choice as to the way in which these powers will be directed.

Mr. Sampson has written eloquently of a Circe-aspect to Virgo-Circe, the beautiful witch who changed Ulysses' crew into swine but was baffled by their leader, the ideal wise man of the Greeks.

Certainly the responsibilities of those who possess the power to use nature's secrets have never been more obvious than in these years. But it seems to the present writer that it is Scorpio rather than Virgo that probes into the innermost recesses of nature, and, though some Virginians are selfish and narrow in their interests and sympathies, there is little to justify us (in my view) in relating the evil but glamorous Circe to this somewhat unexciting sign. Nevertheless, ceremonial magic is traditionally ascribed to the 6th house.

CHAPTER VII

THE LAST SIX OR SOUTHERN SIGNS

LIBRA

HERE we enter the second half of the zodiac and commence the signs which, whatever their failings, are never wholly immersed in self. We leave the first half with Virgo, of all the twelve the most self-centred and self-content, " wedded to his work " and desiring above all things to be left alone ; and we enter Libra, the most dependent of the signs, one to which a single life, in every sense of the expression, is an incomplete life.

It has the distinction of being a late comer to the zodiac.

According to S. Elizabeth Hall, in her profoundly interesting and scholarly work *Astrology : the Link between Two Worlds*,* " the Balance is not found on any Mesopotamian monument and is first mentioned in the Greek zodiac by Varro in the first century B.C. It belongs to a later development of astrology, when the original conception of " a circle of animals " seems to be less prominent : it is an intellectual abstraction, expressing the idea of equipoise."

Libra contrasts with its co-sign, Taurus, with which it is in quincunx, in its sense of *yearning*. Taurus is most easily contented of the signs ; Libra is haunted by a sense of exile, of " weeping by the waters of Babylon." If it is happy it is a mild, not a robust, felicity ; always there is an undercurrent of patient endurance, the memory of an ancient wrong, done or suffered. Something in the remote

*Published by J. M. Watkins.

past that went awry, so that ever since nothing has been quite as it should be. Some mysterious happening that the Christian religion calls the Fall, a hint, it would seem to us astrologers, of Saturn's relation to the sign.

In Virgo man is offered the opportunity of physical purification for the marriage of Libra, but, when all should be well, as it was seen to be on the seventh day—a number reminiscent of this sign—the shadow of the Scorpion seems to fall across the path.

Perhaps there is another useful comparison here with the other quincuncial sign, Pisces, in which Venus is exalted. Libra, perhaps, wishes to anticipate the finality of the Fishes and not merely become the day of temporary, but of final, rest. And Scorpio warns it that this cannot be, that much remains to be done. After the toil and drudgery of Virgo repose, certainly, but only for a time.

This connection with repose naturally tends to make Libra appear a lazy sign. When rising there is evident danger of this failing of " acedia "—torpor, sloth, lethargy —which is one of Seven Deadly Sins. Or at least of indifference, *laissez-faire*, the propensity to leave things to others to decide and to do. Yet Sun-in-Libra is not lethargic, but somewhat the reverse, though the Sun suffers its fall here and your Sun-in-Libra is often seen playing second fiddle in fact, though it may be nominally in control. For example, Hindenburg and Ludendorff.

Apart from its love of peace—which in some circumstances becomes a weakness—Libra has the virtue of frankness and honesty. It simulates very badly. Also, it usually fulfils its obligations conscientiously, though it often enters upon engagements that it repents of later and would give much to escape from.

Libra is pontifical—a maker of bridges. It has an instinct for perceiving points of agreement and thus is an excellent middleman or " honest broker." It excels in inducing people of different views and interests to co-operate ; and this, indeed, is said to have been one of Hitler's outstanding powers. It can always see the common interest when others fall to quarrelling over the proper division of spoils.

It has been argued that Hitler could not possibly have been a native of the most easy-going and peace-loving of the signs, especially as he also had the Sun in Taurus. It is said that, in view of certain afflictions, he might have been a bad man, but that he would not have been actively so ; he would have been too indolent, In reply it may be argued that Hitler was not a physically energetic man, or at last not consistently so, and that Libra, as a cardinal-air sign, is often mentally active, whilst much energy may be ascribed to Moon conjunction Jupiter in Capricorn and Mercury in Aries, as also to ruler with Mars and Pluto in parallel to the ascendant.

But it is probable that the true key to the man's dynamic powers lies rather in his prenatal epoch, and without digressing into this controversial field one may suggest that the student should, even if he does not wish to probe the matter further, glance at the aspects prevalent at the end of July, 1888.

Apart from this, it may be recalled that Ptolemy calls the seventh sign Chelae, the Claws (scil. of the scorpion) and it is possible that something of the quality indicated by this title still clings to the last degrees of the sign. Our modern view that each sign consists of precisely 30° is a little too geometrical, perhaps, to ring true : Nature is not so exact.

To return :

As we have said, Libra is an active sign intellectually and is a dreamer of dreams, though in this respect it is probably less poetic and more practical than Pisces. It can avoid the error of overindulgence in useless fantasy and turn its powers to real constructive imagination, as in architecture and social reform. It can plan ahead with clarity and precision.

But the best channel of self-expression for the sign is as a teacher or exponent. It can set forth ideas in simple and direct language, it senses the attitude and capacities of its audience, and adjusts its expression accordingly, whilst its style is conciliatory and pleasing.

As the sign of reciprocity or mutuality it has a keen sense of justice. The child that complains readily that something "isn't fair" is usually strongly under Libra. In this way there is a close link with Capricorn, as would be expected from the exaltation of Saturn in Libra. But Capricorn aims at order as an ideal, whilst Libra seeks to establish rights and obligations first, as a necessary prerequisite to true order. Order without justice is mere rigidity and is likely to lead to the violence of Aries and final autocracy. In the exercise of justice Libra needs the virtues of Virgo, for, to determine rights, a careful and painstaking collection and sifting of facts is necessary. Libra, of itself, is too prone to compromise, because this is an easy way out ; but a compromise too readily reached may satisfy neither party and hinder a final settlement of differences.

Compromise is regarded nowadays as a distinctively British virtue. Whether this is to be related to the rising of Libra in our 1801 map, I do not know, but earlier generations of the English were not gifted in this way. Elizabeth spoke of her subjects as "unruly beasts" and foreigners of that period described us in terms that are applicable only to a very Mars race. In the horoscope for the Statute of Westminster the sign Libra is untenanted ; but Venus is strong, being in Capricorn in conjunction with the Moon and Mercury, in trine to Neptune but in square to Uranus.

The relation between Libra and marriage is established by ancient tradition and is obvious. This is but a particularly important specialisation of its function of mutuality. In this sign, therefore, that great work, the harmonious relation of the Positive and the Negative, should be achieved. Actual sexual intercourse is probably under the succeeding sign, but that which should proceed this act, the flowing together of two personalities in mutual affection and understanding, is definitely Libran. The exercise of the Scorpio sex-function without regard to the Libran preparation is mere animality ; indeed, many animals indulge in love-play, which may be thought to arouse emotional harmony in terms of the creature concerned, prior to copulation.

Actually, of course, many men have feminine horoscopes and many women have masculine ones, to a greater or less degree, and in this way complications arise. Hence are derived the hen-pecked husband and the wife that " wears the breeches." Or, again, there are cases where both partners are predominantly masculine or predominantly feminine. Fourthly, there are the cases wherein physical and horoscopic sex agree.

Bodies in Libra strongly affect the married life, as much perhaps, as if they were in the 7th house, and this is true to some extent even of the slow-moving planets that remain for a long time in one sign. But in this case the effects are often characteristic of a whole sub-generation and its attitude to wedded life. If, however, the planet in Libra be closely configured with one of the Lights or with Venus or occupies an angle, the individual may be clearly characterised.

However, the subject of marriage demands a treatise of its own. We point out that the principles of Libra are the ideals of a happy and satisfying union.

Yet the sign cannot monopolise the love-emotion. Far

from it. Libra is, in fact, not an intensely emotional sign. Its happiness in love is based on the satisfaction of a conscious or unconscious sense of deficiency, which only a complementary partner can fulfil. The word appropriate to its emotional life is perhaps affection, the Greek Philia. Love, as an emotion that longs to give, is solar. In Libra there is always the sense of moderation that is related to the Saturnian exaltation. Indeed, Libra is the sign of the Golden Mean, of " nothing in excess."

To contrast Libra with Aries is hardly necessary, for the point is obvious. The most self-reliant of the signs learns that it must contact others, and in Libra the ideal principles of reciprocity are portrayed. Adam meets Eve, and loves her.

SCORPIO

This sign has a bad name in traditional astrology, for the ancients considered that the negative sign ruled by any planet always manifested the worst side of that body. Thus, all the bad things that could be ascribed to Mars were attributed to Scorpio. Aries was courageous ; Scorpio brutal and treacherous.

Modern astrologers have almost completely discarded this theory and research has justified their doing so. An examination of 34 cases of violent crime* (admittedly an insufficient number, but nevertheless enough to merit consideration) shows that the number of bodies in Scorpio is actually below the average, whilst a Scorpio ascendant is frequent in cases of outstanding success. It seems well, in any discussion of this sign, to begin with a clearing of its character.

Scorpio contrasts with its opposite, Taurus, in that it signifies power derived from character as against power

*See the author's *Some Principles of Horoscopic Delineation.*

based on possessions. It denotes the *interior* strength of
the nature. In youth the Scorpio is often, as beseems a
watery sign, diffident, shy and retiring, but as its sense of
inner energy and ability unfolds, the story may take a very
different turn.

Often it appears to possess an actual magical or at least
magnetic power of personality, but, apart from this, it has
a persistence, industry and keenness that carry it far,
especially if the lessons of the two preceding signs (physical
purity and moral principle) have been digested. In some
respects it is reminiscent of Virgo, with which, according
to legend, it was at one time united, the sign Libra not
having at that time been introduced into the zodiac. It
has the same desire to know and understand physical
processes. But whereas Virgo is usually constructive and
seeks to make things, Scorpio loves to analyse and dissect.
It tends to pursue the infinitely small as Sagittarius
reaches out to the infinitely large.   Both Virgo and
Scorpio possess unlimited patience in the pursuit of their
aims, but Scorpio as a general rule is provided with greater
physical stamina and courage.

Its weakness is usually of a psychological character and
in particular a fear of things beyond the physical, towards
which, in its investigations, it often approaches and with
which, as a water sign, it has a natural affinity. It does not
fear death as simple physical dissolution, but it fears what
death may bring. It is often fascinated by, and sometimes
dreads, the secrets of the " undiscovered country, from
whose bourn no traveller returns " ; Shakespeare, indeed,
who tells us so little of himself, returns to this note with
such persistence that a Scorpionic, or Plutonic, emphasis
probably occurs in his natus. Macbeth's physical courage
and abject terror of the unknown strike the same note.

It is the sign of tragedy—the tragedy, that is, which
results from evil acts, and which smacks of retribution.

The tragedy that is the result of the operations of fate—
the tragedy, let us say, of " Tess "—can scarcely be placed
under Mars, but is rather Saturnian. Often, of course,
the two are intermingled. One cannot gainsay the
existence of this sombre element in the life of the sign. It
occurs in all three members of the water trigon. But in
Cancer it is the tragedy of the mother weeping over her
children, that of the tribe, family or nation ; or perhaps
an instinctive timidity and general sense of the sorrowful
aspect of life. In Scorpio it is a personal tragedy, that of
the strong man borne down by that which is yet stronger,
the swimmer that sinks in the waves. Thus William
Cowper wrote one of his most poignant poems under the
title " The Castaway," in which he compares his own
spiritual plight with that of a sailor washed overboard :

" No voice divine the storm allay'd,
    No light propitious shone,
When, snatch'd from all effectual aid,
    We perish'd, each alone :
But I beneath a rougher sea,
    And whelm'd in deeper gulfs than he."

The poet's horoscope, given in Maurice Wemyss'
valuable *More Notable Nativities*, shows Mercury in
Scorpio in trine to Saturn. The hour is unknown.

The four elements repeat themselves successively in the
zodiac and each series ends with a sign of water. Each
of three stages, then, ends with water, which may be interpreted as showing either failure, or lustration for the next
step forward. The failure may even be that of death.
Actually, as I have pointed out elsewhere,* Jupiter-
Neptune is more truly representative of death than
any other bodies, and W. H. Sampson considers that
Scorpio relates only to untimely demise. Perhaps Mars-
Pluto-Scorpio represents the destructive factor, and

*In *Symbolic Directions in Modern Astrology*.

Jupiter-Neptune-Pisces the liberation of the life, of the soul in fact. My own experience is that the Jupiter-Neptune factor is involved even in violent death, but not this alone. But if Mr. Sampson's theory is correct, then it is not difficult to see why Scorpio obtained the title of the death-sign in periods when natural death was rare. Indeed, it is not common nowadays if by natural death we mean a tranquil falling asleep and a peaceful return, so far as the body is concerned, to Mother Nature. Such, certainly, *should* be the Jupiter-Neptune dissolution, but in actual practice it is not always so.

But, passing from the problems of physical death, Scorpio is certainly the end of a phase, the second phase, in the zodiacal circle. That which began in the splendour of Leo with its godlike endowments, which toiled with Virgo and reposed with Libra, is tested to the uttermost in Scorpio. Here is the Dark Night of the Soul, as the mystics put it, when the light of Leo has been left far behind, and the works of Virgo and the peace of Libra are no longer sufficient. There is, as the orientals might say, a reaping of karma, good and bad, and usually, the sowing of fresh actions in karmic soil. The life that began in Aries has now run its middle course. It may enter hell, abandon hope as the souls in Dante were bidden to do, and revel in all sorts of devilry ; or it may grit its teeth and press on. We, as astrologers, do at least know there *is* a beyond at this stage.

Of McDougall's primary instincts, Pugnacity, with the correlated emotion anger, or Repulsion with the emotion of disgust, seem most like the sign now under discussion, and preferably the latter, as being negative in character.

Certainly, amongst the deadly sins of the theologians, Scorpio recalls Pride. In a sense there is a pride of each of the four fixed signs ; Taurus, pride of possession ; Leo, pride of sheer exuberant vitality, or, decadently, pride in pomp and circumstance ; Scorpio, a bitter pride, arising from envy, or at least accompanied by it, and Aquarius, pride of knowledge or intellectual conceit. Scorpionic pride is so deep that it is hard to understand. One can see the wealth of Taurus, the grandeur of Leo, the book-cases and laboratories that represent the knowledge of Aquarius; and although one may not consider that they are matters for pride, yet one can recognise that they are there and that they are in some sense unusual. But with the pride of Scorpio it is often difficult to see where the basis lies even for a mistaken self-esteem. Milton says that Satan had a " sense of injured merit " but we are nowhere, so far as I am aware, enlightened as to what that merit was, or why Satan deemed it insufficiently appreciated. Certainly, down to this very day, one sometimes finds the children of Scorpio descanting upon the same topic and refusing to be comforted. If Cancer often weeps, so Scorpio often curses.

The true expression of this quality is self-respect, arising from appreciation of the worth of character ; and the native of Scorpio who presents a picture of self-respect, even if there is a touch of aloofness, probably affords the pleasantest example of the sign, so far as personality is concerned.

Finally we may contrast Scorpio with the quincuncial signs Aries and Gemini, if only to observe how unalike they are. Aries is self-expression ; Scorpio is self-control, self repression. Gemini chatters away with the " innocence of childhood pure " ; Scorpio sits aside and broods.

So much for the four signs of the Individual.

SAGITTARIUS

Here we reach the third great creative impulse of Fire, expressed in mental terms under the rulership of Jupiter.

Under Aries man received the impulse to act—*im Anfang war die Tat*. Under Leo he learnt to love, that is, to give of himself. In Sagittarius he must prepare to receive and proclaim the truth. Not the factual and analytic truths of Mercury, but the all-comprehensive truths of cosmic principles and the Divine Wisdom. He must fit himself to be the sage and prophet, the intellectual illuminator and initiator of mankind. He must unfold the powers of true intuition, the direct perception of universal truths.

A good deal has been made of the centaur-symbol, as indicating a half-bestial nature, man arising from the brute. I regard this as an erroneous interpretation. All fire-signs have a lower expression in what may be fairly called high spirits or animal exuberance ; and your primitive Sagittarian may be fond of horse-play and the stories of the smoking-room. As much might, *mutatis mutandis*, be said of the Ram or Lion. The myth of the centaurs was probably based on the first appearance, to a race that had never before beheld them, of men mounted on horse-back. But Chiron was the instructor of the Grecian heroes, a truly Sagittarian figure of venerable wisdom, one who transmits to the most worthy of mankind the wisdom of the Gods. And the symbol of the Ninth Sign refers, it is believed, to Chiron and not to the centaurs generally, whose reputation was somewhat reminiscent of the rougher sort of Sagittarian. They were, in fact, drunken rioters.

So splendid is the true expression of this sign, so glorious its mission, that one may be pardoned for wondering what can lie beyond to be achieved. It may well be said that the sage or prophet, in the highest sense of these words, is man at his pinnacle of expression. He is man the representative of the Gods. What more can he become ?

The answer must be that this sign is clearly the completion of man's evolution in terms of fire ; but that he must also achieve completion in terms of the three other elements.   And the vital endowment is not the end of man's destiny, but the beginning.   Life is given to be used, and this is as true of spiritual life as of any other.

Sagittarius is certainly a vital sign in every sense and it does not keep its talents buried.   It is restless, mentally and physically.   What it has, it loves to impart.   Hence it is not only generous or even prodigal with money, but it is also the general mentor, the preacher, the adviser.   Herein lie two dangers.   First of all, a preacher should be certain that he really has something useful to say and has the right to say it.   Otherwise he is a mere windbag, proffering counsel to those who are as wise and virtuous as himself, or more so.   The love of " getting on their hindlegs " and giving good advice is strong in both Jovian signs ; to do so flatters the natural man and for that very reason it is a temptation to his vanity.   Those who are truly qualified to offer good advice to others, except in specialised subjects, are necessarily few.

This propensity appears, in one of its lowest forms, as the Sagittarian racing tipster.   What a gulf, from the saint to the tipster !   Yet, down from the highest to the lowest, there is the same tendency—to give advice.

Naturally the Jovian proclivity towards hypocrisy has scope here : if one has no real " inside information " to impart, one is tempted to pretend to possess it.

As the share pusher or tipster of the racecourse offers a short cut to wealth, so we have various cults that represent themselves as having the secret of some short-cut way to esoteric powers and knowledge.   There are, of course, none such.

Similarly the well-recognised hopefulness of Sagittarius

has its higher and lower forms. There is an optimism based on philosophical argument—indeed the original use of this much abused word is ascribed to Leibnitz, who deduced from the postulate of a Perfect Being the theory that all creation must be likewise perfect. In the words of George Macdonald " What we call evil, is the only and best shape which, for the person and his condition at the time, could be assumed by the best good."

At its worst, this hopefulness is the mad obsession of the gambler that " his luck will turn."

Sagittarius contrasts with Gemini in its profuseness and carelessness, both fire characteristics. Gemini is a teacher of facts and figures, exact and precise ; Sagittarius is a teacher of ideas and theories. It seeks to get beyond the already ascertained, which satisfies Gemini, into the unknown and unexplored. Physically it is not by any means always the great traveller that tradition describes, but mentally it is a perpetual voyager into uncharted seas. Hard facts are confining things, and the sign hates confinement.

It is a good natural psychologist and likes to study human nature, having a more alive approach to the subject than the Saturnian signs.

It contrasts sharply with the quincuncial signs, its recklessness being the reverse of Cancerian timidity and its restlessness with Taurean contentment and staticism.

R. L. Stevenson gave voice to a true Sagittarian sentiment when he wrote that " to travel hopefully is a better thing than to arrive." Incompletion is characteristic of the sign and that, since it is the symbol of cosmic progress, is as it should be. Air and Earth can see their tasks completed in perfection, witness the triumphs of Greek statuary, but Water must ebb and flow, even when it has reached the ocean of Pisces, and in Sagittarius there is the unending flare and flicker of the upward tending flames.

CAPRICORNUS

Sagittarius, the first of the universal signs as W. H. Sampson has called them, is a happy influence. Fire, indeed, becomes happier as it progresses through the circle. Universality does not come uncongenially to Spirit, but the reverse. Far otherwise is it with Earth. Taurus is regarded as the most contented of the twelve ; Virgo is looked upon as prone to fuss and fidget ; Capricorn is stigmatised as melancholic and despondent.

This old attribution is doubtless exaggerated, but the reason for discontent is not far to seek, though we cannot dispose of the matter by simply saying " The sign is ruled by Saturn." Earth is by nature self-regarding and limited. In Taurus the wants are few and are such as Mother Nature can provide in return for simple works, laborious rather than vexatious. Virgo is still in the first half of the zodiac, but it is at the end of that sector and is fretted by the sense of responsibilities that lie ahead and horizons that will broaden when the old familiar landscape is all that is desired. In Capricorn the self-regarding tendency *has* to face up to the problems of collective life, or else fall back, as some Capricorns do fall back, into a self-centred and selfish life that should have been outgrown. Those who take this path usually make a dismal end. They are perhaps Mr. Dombeys, swollen with the conception of their own unique importance, or else they are discontented pushers and climbers, fretting at what they consider their failure to obtain due recognition and envious of others.

Capricorn rising, indeed, is often very different from the traditional picture, at once less efficient and more likeable. The musical gift is often, for example, quite prominent and in fact they are frequently highly cultured people, and in no sense worldly. Frequently they are not success-ful in mundane matters and exhibit a propensity for taking hold of sticks by the wrong ends, so far as ordinary life is concerned. The attribute of cunning may appear in low types, but it has rarely come to my notice, and when it does make an appearance it is often of the kind that would decieve no one, by reason of its ineptitude.

Sun in Capricorn conforms more to the usual picture, prudent, conservative and ambitious. Mercury is extremely well placed in the sign and often shows much ability for dealing with the world of affairs.

The interest in politics shows the movement towards a universalisation of the earth-principle. It is derived from the innate desire to produce mundane perfection upon as wide a scale as possible. Naturally the conception of perfection may be, or at any rate seem to most people to be, based upon totally wrong ideas. That would apply to Hitler, with his Moon-Jupiter in this sign. But the vision of a New Order is true Capricorn, however faulty the actualisation may be.

Faced with this vision of the universal perfection of the mundane order, Capricorn is doubtless often despondent, for we are far from realising anything of the sort, and the defects of our existing circumstances are patent and close at hand. He is apt, too, being under Saturn, to conceive of perfection in too static a sense, as something resulting from a general disciplining and controlling. Prussianism, in fact. If the lessons of Sagittarius are properly learned, this error will not arise.

The stern, fateful, almost gloomy side of the sign seems to me to have been exaggerated. It is true, of course, that we can contrast the kindly and sympathetic Cancer with the strict duty-loving Capricorn ; but in actual fact Capricornian parents are (so far as my observation goes) as affectionate as any, and more aware of the responsibilities of parenthood than many others. Indeed, they take these very much to heart. Similarly, though erratic and capricious in many things, once married they are usually devoted and conscientious partners.

Capricorn is also called a diabolic sign, sharing this distinction with Scorpio. Both signs tend to produce pride, certainly. But in attributing devilish qualities to Capricorn I cannot but think that astrologers are in fact exemplifying another and more attractive aspect, that of the universal scapegoat who takes upon his shoulders the sins of the people. I would think that, granted the existence of diabolic powers and entities, they do not limit their activities to two signs only, but have a technique adapted to the natives of all of them! The temptation of the Scorpion might lie in the almost magical powers which, as we have already written, it often possesses and which sometimes deliver weaker persons into its hands, as Faustus into those of Mephistopheles. The Capricorn temptation is (as has frequently been asserted) that of earthly power and dominion. But surely this is a symbolic truth not always exemplified in actuality. In real life the Saturnian man seldom has the offer of pomp and circumstance on easy terms presented to him ; he is found working patiently for whatever he gets. Nor, so far as I can observe, is he usually at all indignant at this necessity ; it is Sagittarius, not the maligned Goat, that likes easy money.

The Jews are principally under Capricorn and they are accused of liking short cuts to fortune. Whether this is really the case, I cannot say ; I should have said that, as a race, they are singularly industrious. Yet the New Testament does contain condemnations of the leaders of Jewry that certainly sound like attacks upon the traditional Capricorn—the love of high places, hypocritical formalism in religion, the desecration of holy places in pursuit of gain.

Countries ruled by Capricorn tend to exhibit the caste

system in one form or another. The British (the Sun is in Capricorn in two of our three suggested national horoscopes) are regarded as snobbish. This tendency is part of the love of order that is inborn in the sign.

We have already mentioned the perfectionism of the better types of Capricorn. This applies also to their moral life—and that of others, for they are apt to be hard judges of themselves and of their neighbours.

They are often highly introspective and scrutinise their acts and motives in a manner that seems morbid to more highly vitalised types   There is indeed something aquatic about Capricorn, the goat which is its symbol often being portrayed as half a fish.*   In the order of the planets outwards from the Sun (placing the planetoids over Virgo) Capricorn falls to Neptune ; and there are distinct signs that this assignment is not altogether inept.†

Perhaps it is its tendency to self-centredness combined with its perfectionism which so often makes Capricorn displeased with itself and with others, and, as a result, causes it to be frugal in praise and correspondingly unpopular. It is a bad encourager.

Its ideal expression, in active life, would probably be in the Civil or Consular Services, Universities, government offices and great and substantial commercial houses. It makes an excellent accountant. Balance sheets and blue books would be an appropriate pabulum. But this should be taken as referring rather to persons with important bodies in the sign, rather than to those with it on the ascendant, these being, as we have tried to emphasise,

*S. Elizabeth Hall, in *Astrology: the Link between Two Worlds*, points out that the last three signs have each an aquatic connection, which she ascribes to the Sun being in them during the Mesopotamian watery season. She associates Aquarius with the idea of deluge.

†Thus also, Venus is well-placed in Cancer, Mars is particularly strong in Leo, Jupiter is said to " joy " in Libra, Saturn in Scorpio is exceptionally powerful, and Uranus shows similarities with Sagittarius —notably the dislike of control.

very different, more restless and obviously cardinal, more friendly, and less dignified.

AQUARIUS

It might well be expected that the two signs ruled (according to tradition) by Saturn would be the easiest of all the twelve to understand. Yet this is not so ; we have already indicated the contradictions that arise in regard to Capricorn, in so many cases typified by the University don or the efficient civil servant and yet so often discontented, capricious and uncertain, the evident victim of unsatisfied emotional cravings.

It is equally difficult to place Aquarius under one definite type ; and this perhaps might be expected from the symbol, which, strangely, introduces the idea of flowing water into a sign which is properly fixed air.

As the last of the airy trigon the Waterman should represent the final result of man's mental unfoldment. As such, it should be the scientist and the artist in his more intellectual expressions. Not so much the scientist who is directly concerned with nature—that would rather fall to Capricorn, as being of earth—but the higher mathematician, the man who deals in symbols and the ideas they indicate. Up to a point this seems correct.

But Aquarius has a noticeable propensity to sociology, and, as a means towards the practical aspects of this science, to politics. It is, indeed, apparently more inclined to politics than is Capricorn, at least in these days. But it may be surmised that the underlying motive is quite different. Capricorn is a natural politician or statesman, for careers such as these promise satisfaction for its ambitions and also for its innate desire to arrange and ordinate wherever it can. It would seem, however, that the Aquarian is drawn to such things by a genuine desire to benefit mankind.

We may admit that the talk of Aquarian brotherhood and brotherliness may well contain exaggeration, at least in the manner in which it is often expressed by the fanciful and emotional. But Aquarius can cite a very long catalogue of men and women who have been true lovers of their kind and have worked in politics and in literature to help the down-trodden. They were, in fact, idealists, though sometimes mistaken ones.

This characteristic is not perhaps shown by the Saturnian rulership or even by the oft-asserted affinity between Uranus and Aquarius ; but it is plainly signified by the symbol of the man pouring water from his urn. It *may* also have some relation to the fact that in our latitudes, Aquarius rising means Pisces intercepted in the first house and that a person born with the Sun in Aquarius will usually spend an important part of his life with the pro-gressed luminary in the Fishes. But the fact stands : Aquarius is a great worker for the good of mankind, not as a rule, in private charity, but in politics (F. D. Roosevelt, Abraham Lincoln) or in letters (Robert Burns, Charles Dickens).

We are said, of course, to be living in, or at any rate to be approaching the " Aquarian Age." That is to say, the vernal equinox, retrograding through the zodiacal constellations, is said to be in or near the confines of the constellation Aquarius, which is presumed to be of a similar nature to that of the corresponding sign. Only, as the boundaries of the constellations are uncertain (unless we accept the apparently arbitrary delimitations of modern astronomers) it is impossible to say, within many years, when this has happened, or will happen.

It is certain that a very strong Aquarian influence became apparent in human affairs at the close of the 18th century, as in the American and French revolutions, the industrial revolution, and the Romantic revival. This may

be ascribed to the discovery of Uranus, but it may also
have been the beginning of an Aquarian Age or Sub-Age.

When we come to consider the more ordinary types of
Aquarius we find them sociable but often somewhat
detached emotionally, frequently interested in music or
science, and fond of wild nature, This last, indeed is an
outstanding Aquarian trait, which seems at variance with
fixed air, but is quite undeniable.

It is to be observed that it is not always forsaken
humanity that appeals to the Aquarian, but also out-of-
the-way and neglected mental pursuits. The words of
Cleanthes' Hymn to Zeus " things not dear to man are dear
to Thee " might with slight alteration—most men for
man—be applied to the Aquarian.

Just as many regard Capricorn as untrustworthy and
deceptive, so some accuse the natives of Aquarius of being
undependable. It is true that they often act strangely
amd seem to belie their high ideals in their actions. They
seem subject to whims and fancies that perplex and sometimes vex others. The farmers who purchased copies of
Ruskin's *Notes on the Construction of Sheepfolds* must
have felt that they had been dishonestly misled when they
found that the work in question was a plea for a union of
churches. Possibly Ruskin did not foresee this, but in any
case the joke, if such it was, increased his royalties and
laid him open to cynical attacks as a consequence.

Are they really children of Uranus ?

Some astrologers, especially in America, seem to take
this almost for granted, and one can think of Aquarians who
had a close resemblance to the hot-tempered, rebellious,
intensely freedom-loving Uranian. Conversely, there are
Uranians well known to me who have the friendly ways of
the sign and only manifest their love of personal liberty in
adopting a few mild eccentricities. Generally Uranus is
more intense than Aquarius; he has stronger likes and

dislikes ; he is less judicial and detached, and, when rising, he confers a swarthy complexion unlike the Saturnian pallor of most adult Aquarians. We may safely regard the attribution as far from proven, a clear case of jumping to conclusions, and yet not by any means obviously wrong.

It is noteworthy that a good many soldiers are born with Aquarius rising, though not with the Sun in that sign. This may have some relation to the gregarious life of the service man, and also perhaps to the fact that when Aquarius rises Scorpio is on the " natural " tenth, if it may so be termed.

Aquarius is distinctly the sign of collective man, as Leo stands for individual man, and the problem of our days is to reconcile the two conceptions, society and the individual. One is sometimes disturbed when one sees some caricature of the " Little Man " as a frightened rabbit-like person, pathetically pleased with little things and clearly living in fear of his life, lest he come into conflict with one or other of the thousand regulations that have been set to keep him in order. Why has the robust John Bull, who represented our grandfathers, given place to this poor little creature ? Because of the advent of the vaunted Aquarian Age, or something much like it !

The Age of Aquarius will bring its problems, as the others have done. The preservation of a reasonable amount of personal liberty will be one of them. There is this paradox about the sign that it seems to love mankind and yet does not always understand humanity as composed of living, loving, struggling individuals. Just as an astrologer may forget, as he studies his charts, that a living soul is behind them, each and everyone. It is perhaps distressing to the Aquarian town-planner that so many people would rather live in a more or less insanitary cottage than in the finest block of modern flats, and that a mother who has to fetch every drop of water half a mile from the village pump will often keep her children far cleaner than one who has it laid on, h. and c., in every room. The strangeness of the human soul has puzzled many students. However, in this period Aquarius has it by the scruff of the neck, figuratively speaking, and intends to teach it to live, or exist, *Plangemäss*.

But the cream of the paradox is that Aquarius is often not only the planner, but also the most vigorous opponent of being subjected to planning, a mysterious sign indeed.

Russia, that Aquarian country which in our own times has passed from autocratic muddle to an equally despotic planning, where thousands of families are uprooted and sent hundreds of miles away just as a farmer may move a flock of sheep to a fresh field because it needs manuring, may yet provide us with further dramatic developments of the Message of the Waterbearer.

" Behold, I make all things new ! " seems the note of Aquarius.

PISCES

In passing from Aquarius to the Fishes one notes a great difference : the latter sign has Humility. It is perhaps somwhat sad that, after starting from the self-reliant and confident Aries, one closes the circle, after so many adventures, on a note of so different a pitch.

The advanced native of the Fishes, to use the phrase commonly employed in such connections, is perhaps a saint or even an illuminatus, a true mystic. Or he maybe a hermit or the inhabitant of a monastery, living a godly life. The Path of Devotion appeals to many Pisceans.

So does the Path of Beauty ; the sign produces artists, and in particular painters, as well as many poets, especially mystical poets and poets of the sea. Above all, actors.

Again (though this is not a profession as a rule) it is the Good Samaritan of the zodiac, extending its loving ministrations not only to human beings but also to animals. However, it must be added that Pisceans are also often devotees of the rod, that particularly deceptive and Neptunian form of sport.

Among the ordinary run of people Pisceans often go to sea ; and they are also attracted to the liquor and drug trades and to forms of chemical research that have to do with drugs, fermentation, and so forth.

They make good spies and detectives.

What is the root-idea of this strange sign ?

If the relation of Uranus to Aquarius is uncertain, that of the Fishes to Neptune is not. The planet may not rule the sign but beyond all question there is a close affinity here. In exact opposition to Aries, which insists on itself, Pisces loves to assume all shapes, like the old sea-god Proteus, and to lose itself—its self—in them. Chesterton told us that God is a great jester and wrote that most Neptunian—or Piscean—joke, *The Man that was Thursday*. What a cosmic jest have we here ! After our zodiacal peregrination, we find ourselves in Pisces, slipping out of one coat into another, a Joey-the-Clown sort of ending.

Not content with outward changes the Piscean often experiments, through drugs and stimulants, to change his inner self as well. Or he may do this in day-dreams in which he sees himself play all sorts of parts in the drama of an imaginary life.

He is easily elated and easily depressed ; that is natural enough, because mutable water will be like that. Whether he is sociable or not depends chiefly on Saturn ; your Saturnian Piscean may be an anchorite, but if Jupiter prevails he may be a most convivial fellow, much less particular about his associates than Aquarius, who is something of an intellectual snob in practice, though not in theory. Aquarius thinks of his fellows as " types " or " classes " but to Pisces they are eminently living beings, from whom one can borrow when in need and to whom one will also gladly impart financial assistance, if one can, when they are in difficulties.

In one sense Pisces is more friendly than Aquarius. That is to say, he is much more hail-fellow-well-met. He delights in play the host and is an excellent inn-keeper, delighting in extending hospitality and enjoying it.

For the present, Pisces is somewhat out of place. He does not fit in with the modern worship of efficiency, and the self-help principles of the last century were not to his taste either. One cannot picture an age more to his liking than that of Chaucer, when a pilgrimage to the shrine of a saint, with plenty of genial conversation and the interchange of amusing narratives would have suited him excellently. He suffered a sad set-back when Henry VIII dissolved the monasteries, in which he might have been an inmate or of which he might be a dependent. The Piscean influence appears again on the stage of history, in sorry plight, when the great gin-drinking plague ravaged England in the 18th century and had to be suppressed, after it had wrought terrible injury. Lastly, Pisces appears again, soon after the discovery of Neptune in 1846. In 1848 modern spiritualism came into being after the fraudulent phenomena of the Fox Sisters, who were instigated, by the way, by an elder married sister named Fish !

Pisces is the sign of Transformation. And it closes the zodiacal circle. What, then, will be the final transformation and what succeeds it ? We shall all be transformed, wrote St. Paul, in the twinkling of an eye.

For the body, we know, the final transformation will be that of death ; and here there is no mystery. But beyond?

We know the words of one of the most truly Piscean characters in all literature :

" something after death,
The undiscovered country from whose bourn
No traveller returns."

Plato tells us that the souls drink of the waters of Lethe, some very deeply some less, and Pisces, which often has a weak memory for earthly things, seems paradoxically to be a sign which does not altogether lose the memory of heaven when it descends to earth. Hence its restlessness and its eagerness to try ever-various shapes and forms of experience, seeking to recapture Below what it has seen Above. It is a sacred quest, the quest for the Holy Grail. Unfortunate, if it goes to the wine cup instead of that sacred chalice ; but if it is a ready sinner, it is a quick forgiver ; there is no malice in Pisces.

So, it is as the Final Absolution that I would take leave of Pisces.

In *Iphigeneia in Tauris* Euripides makes the heroine say :

" The sea doth wash all the world's ills away "

So, then, we may close with the view that Pisces is Dissolution, but also Absolution.

Capricorn is the sign which feels the burden of sin. Its attitude to the problems of the soul are apt to be clouded with this. It tends to doctrines of fate and predestination, or of the strict retributive justice of *karma*. Aquarius often rejects the conception of individual responsibility altogether and blames a man's failings upon the social order. Pisces humbly admits its sins and delinquencies and seeks forgiveness. It cries not for justice, but for mercy.

It would seem that the zodiacal circle ends with this declaration of faith in the Eternal Mercy.

It is not for us to speculate as to the answer.

CHAPTER VIII

PROBLEMS OF THE HOUSES

In theory the Houses are said to qualify the final precipitation of the stellar values and finally canalise them into one or more of the Departments into which life is divided and which they severally represent.

But this rule, simple in statement, is not simple in application. For one thing, the average aspect involves, through occupancy and rulership, several houses. Venus square Mars for example will usually affect two houses by occupancy and four by rulership, even omitting their natural lordship over Taurus, Libra, Aries and Scorpio and their consequent affinity with the corresponding houses. In practice this may be to some extent simplified by one of the planets occupying the same house that it rules, and so forth. But nevertheless it must be obvious that a method that is so wide in its scope must be virtually useless, at least in a case such as the above.

Furthermore, it is difficult to distinguish between the values of the signs and of the houses. The rule that the former relate to "soul" and the latter to "body" may have some theoretical basis but it is of little use in practice. House-positions may affect character in a very marked degree ; this is indeed generally acknowledged in regard to the 1st house and probably the 3rd and 9th also. Sign-positions may produce effects in terms of circumstance. This perhaps is less generally admitted, but it is true. The writer has known, for example, cases wherein malefics in Leo have given almost endless trouble through children, though the 5th house was in no way involved.

Similarly with Taurus and financial conditions, and so on.

These difficulties in using the houses have caused some schools (though not in this country) to eliminate the domal idea from their astrology, except for the angles, of which the importance can scarcely be denied by any intelligent student.

The present writer, in studying the mundane maps of the war years, found that house-influence was only sharply and unmistakably shown when bodies were exactly on cusps ; otherwise it was vague. But it is not suggested that this would be true in the case of nativities. Most mundane figures last only for a limited period but our natus is with us throughout life and there is plenty of time for minor values to be expressed clearly enough to be apparent.

Zodiacal positions change slowly ; and if we were to omit the houses, we should find that all people born anywhere over a period of several hours would have virtually identical " horoscopes," which would reduce our art almost to a wraith. Again, horary astrology, which some students use with great success, depends greatly upon the houses.

The fact that there has been, for centuries, much difference of opinion about the true system of domification is itself an argument that the problem is not a simple one ; there has been no similar doubt about the number and dimensions of the signs.

The question of house-division or domification has been treated in Alan Leo's *Astrology for All : Part Two* as well as in innumerable articles both in this country, in France, in Germany, and in the United States. Yet no final conclusion has been reached, perhaps because the disputants, almost without exception, have confined themselves to the theory of the matter and have eschewed the production of well-authenticated cases that might have proved the correctness of their views. For this purpose, it is obvious that mundane maps should be used, since their timing cannot be called into doubt.*

There are systems for employing astrology in connection with horse-racing in which the use of the exact cusp is deemed essential and one might, therefore, expect a decision from this branch. Yet students can be found who claim, perhaps rather too confidently, that they have achieved excellent results, some with one, some with another, system of houses.†

In view of the fact that, as we have said, the subject has been very fully ventilated already, we will only attempt here to give a brief survey of the chief methods still to a greater or less extent in vogue.

The method of equal house division, sometimes ascribed to Ptolemy, is hardly a true method of domification. It takes the ascendant (i.e., the intersection of the horizon by the ecliptic) as the cusp of the first house, and then adds 30° of longitude for each successive cusp, counting the midheaven, which will not of course necessarily coincide with the cusp of the 10th house, as a sort of Point of Honour.

This system has the advantage of not collapsing in high latitudes and often seems, in natal astrology, to give excellent results, simple though it is.

Porphyry, who lived about a century later than Ptolemy, divided the mundane sphere into four quadrants by the

*See observations on the 1946 vernal equinox in the September issue of *Astrology* for that year ; this figure appeared to be a strong argument in favour of Campanus' method.

†An *exact* aspect to the cusp of the 5th will often correspond in a striking manner with the name of a winning horse. Thus, in a case wherein Saturn in Cancer was in precise trine to cusp 5 (Placidus) the winner was named *Capricorn*, the second was *Master Builder* ! Cases could be multiplied. *Airborne* won the Derby when cusp 5 was trine Uranus in Gemini ; *Radiotherapy*, a very Uranian name, was third,

horizon and meridian, a purely mundane conception, and then trisected equally the four arcs of the ecliptic within each quadrant. This seems clearly illogical, for, if the horizon and meridian divide the ecliptic unequally, as they may and usually do, why should the succedent and cadent houses be obtained by an equal division ?

This method is used in India, but it must be remembered that near the equator all systems produce very similar results.

Campanus, who lived in the 13th century, obtained his quadrants by means of the meridian and horizon and his secondary houses by circles similarly cutting the north and south points of the horizon and trisecting equally each quadrant of the prime vertical, which is a circle passing through the zenith and nadir and the east and west points of the horizon.

This domification is simple and logical in the extreme and it is, therefore, strange that, until modern times, no one appears to have paid much attention to it.

Regiomontanus lived in the 15th century. His system consists of circles drawn through the north and south points of the horizon, as in the foregoing method ; but they divide the equator, not the prime vertical, into twelve equal arcs. Thus, at the terrestrial equator these two systems produce similar figures, because at the equator the prime vertical and the celestial equator correspond. As one moves north or south from the earth's equator, they draw away from one another.

In these latitudes the Regiomontanian figures differ but little from those in common use to be mentioned below. In theory they are quite different.

This method flourished during the 17th century and was then almost entirely superseded by the method of Placidus, according to which nearly all the tables printed in modern publications are constructed.

However, this system has been fiercely (the adverb is not too strong) attacked on the same grounds as that of Porphyry, i.e., because the angles are determined by one method and the intermediate cusps by another. It is obvious that, except at the equinoxes, the Sun does not rise exactly between midnight and noon : why then, if the horizon is the cusp of the 1st house, should the other cusps be determined by an equal division of the time taken by the Sun to pass from angle to angle ?

However, Placidean tables are in general use and at least nine out of ten students, including many experts, employ them, calculating mundane primary directions by this system and taking note of transits over the Placidean cusps.

Indeed all the methods enumerated here have advocates among experienced and judicious students.

Campanus has been criticised on the grounds that it bears no relation to the earth's rotation, a point which may or may not strike the reader as important. At all events, the present writer considers that its merits should be examined, as far as possible, by every serious astrologer. It seems valuable from the more purely *factual* (as against the psychological) point of view.

On the other hand, the so-called Ptolemaic system often seems to strike deeper, as it were, into the natives' character. Yet it lacks real basis as a method of scientific domification. It is really a secondary method of dividing the zodiac into twelve equal sections, starting from the ascendant instead of from 0° Aries, the introduction of the ascendant being the only truly mundane feature about it.

The present writer has introduced a method of house division which in practice yields very similar results but is quite distinct in theory. In this, the houses are demarcated by circles passing through the celestial poles and dividing the equator into twelve equal arcs, the cusp of the 1st house passing through the ascendant.

This system, therefore, agrees with the natural rotation of the heavens and also produces, as the Ptolemaic does not, distinctive cusps for each house, capable of receiving individually their own aspects.

Since the relation between equator and ecliptic is constant at any one time over the whole earth, one set of tables can be used for the whole world.

This method might be called Equatorial, or, to distinguish it from that of Regiomontanus in which the ebuator is also the basis of division, Poli-Equatorial.

Such a set of tables can easily be constructed. The ascendant must be found in the usual way and with the usual tables ; it is then stated in terms of right ascension by means of the tables given in all books that treat of primary directions, and to it is added 30° of right ascension for each successive cusp. These data must then be re-stated in terms of celestial logitude.*

The results may be tested by reference to radical maps and to directions formed to and by the cusps, radical and progressed, and by transits to cusps.

Thus Edward VII died on 6 May, 1910, when Uranus by transit was in 25 ♑, opposed to natal cusp 8.

Tennyson died when the progressed M.C. was about 11 ♉, yielding under tables for the place of birth, an ascendant of 25 ♏, and an 8th cusp of 27 ♍, square of radical Venus, ruling 12th, and trine radical Saturn in Scorpio in radical 6th, a suitable indication of the death of one who passed full of honours, at an advanced age, and in the spirit of his own poem "Crossing the Bar."

We append three genitures erected by this method.

*A set of tables may be obtained from the author, price 6d. post paid, for those who wish to experiment.

NATIVITY OF KING EDWARD VII

Erected by the Author's Equatorial Method

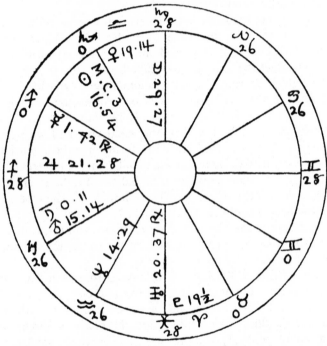

The presence of the Moon, in close square to Saturn, on cusp 10 seems peculiarly appropriate to the native's strict upbringing and suppression by his royal Mother, who refused for many years to allow him to take part in public affairs. Venus in 10th agrees with his popularity and that of his Consort.

By Placidus and Regiomontanus the Moon is within 2° of cusp 9 and by Campanus it is on the line of demarcation between 8th and 9th both of which seem to have little significance.

THE NATIVITY OF EMILY POPEJOY

Erected according to the Author's Method

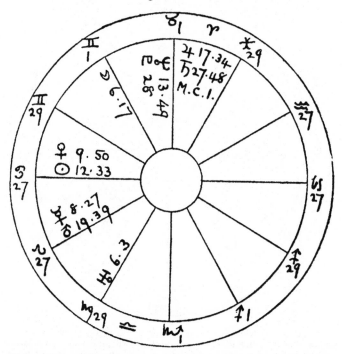

The native of this horoscope, a maidservant, died as the result of ill-treatment at the hands of her mistress. This seems clearly indicated,in principle, by Saturn close to the cusp of the 10th and Neptune, squared by Mars, in that house.

By Placidus Jupiter, well aspected by Mars, is in the 10th followed by Saturn ; by Campanus Jupiter is also in the 10th.

Ruler square Uranus in Virgo in 2nd shows starvation and lack of comforts. By Placidus it is in the 3rd, which is meaningless.

THE NATIVITY OF ALFRED TENNYSON

Erected according to the Equatorial Method

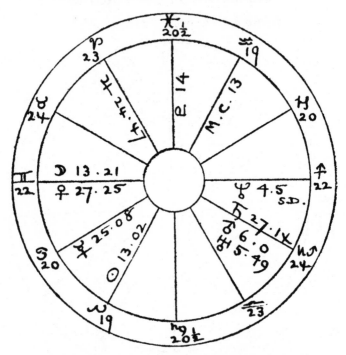

This geniture, when erected according to Placidus or Regiomontanus, shows four malefics in the 6th house, which seems inappropriate to the native's robust health, especially as the Sun, though in dignity and sextile the Moon, is in square to two of them and is 105° from Saturn. Campanus moves Saturn and Neptune into the 7th (if the cusp be taken as the centre) but leaves Mars and Uranus in the 6th. They would be much better placed in the 5th, indicating the emotional tragedy which led to *In Memoriam* and the death of the poet's son of fever. Saturn would hardly affect the health adversely, as it is in trine to Mercury and is contacted by both benefics (admittedly by quincunx) but it agrees with the native's mental qualities and also with his rather forbidding manners in society, despite the rising Venus.

Other points worth noticing are that Jupiter in the 11th seems to agree much better with the poet's phenomenal success than that it should be on the 12th cusp. He won fame, rank and money.

The question of house-orbs is a difficult one. Since we allow no orbs to signs and since we attribute meanings to the houses in correspondence with the signs and in every way treat them as the mundane analogues of these, it appears *prima facie* unreasonable to ascribe any orbs to houses. But practical experience has always postulated something of the kind. Judging solely by this criterion, the author would attribute some 10° of orb to the ascendant and perhaps almost as much to the other angles, whilst the succedent houses might be allowed somewhat less and the cadent houses perhaps 5°. These might be increased slightly for the Sun and Moon.

However, it seems logical to suppose that a body's *main* effect is in the house actually occupied, there being merely an overshadowing of the adjacent cusp. The result will be a " colligation " of the two houses. So that, for example, the Sun in Tennyson's case would indicate money (2nd) through writings (3rd).

As for the contention of some (but not all) advocates of Campanus, that the cusp is the centre of the house, this squares neither with reason nor my experience.

But another point arises here, In the writer's view all bodies in the same sign are, so to speak, drawn together and exert a certain mutual influence, as one might say *per commune signum*, through community of sign. This is probably a good deal weaker than actual conjunction, but it exists. The same principle operates with domal cusps. Thus, if we refer to the maps of Mussolini and Hitler on pages 54, 55, erected by Campanus, we find that the groups in Gemini in the former chart and in Taurus in the latter are actually in the 7th house, which tallies with their aggressions on other states. But they also affect the cusp of the 8th house *per commune signum* and this accords with their violent ends.

This principle may be likened to the manner in which a

NATIVITY OF LANDRU

Erected according to the Method of Campanus

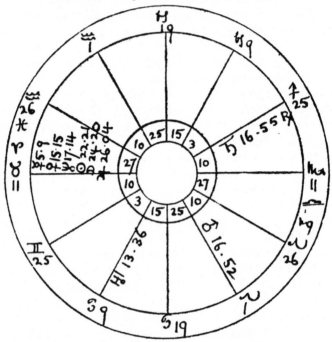

It will be seen that in this extraordinary figure a satellitium of no less than six bodies (includes both Lights) is in Aries. But as the boundary of the house, according to those who take the cusp as the centre of the house, is 27° Pisces, all these are to be considered as in the 1st house. This seems out of keeping with his subtle and treacherous methods. If we reject the " cusps as centres " idea and adopt that which is set out above, we shall say they are operative solely in the 12th because a different sign is on the ascendant, so that it has no sign-community with the satellitium. Were there such, we should still say they were in the 12th and exerted their main effects therein, but we should add that they did to some degree affect the ascendant.

Incidentally this nativity is a good example of the dubious nature of the grand trine and its tendency to interweave the native's life with those of others in a peculiar manner.

Further, it is an example of the perversive operation of Uranus, the principal afflictor in this horoscope.

drop of ink in a tumbler of water slowly spreads throughout the contents. In the same way (except that its principal influence always remains centred at its actual location) the " influence " of the planet percolates through the sign, but not beyond, except in terms of the acknowledged doctrine of orbs.

We refer in this connection to the horoscope of Landru, the notorious French bride-murderer, who lured numerous women to death by promises of matrimony, the motive being avarice.

It is of course a matter for regret that astrologers have been unable to assert with unanimity that one method of house division is right, and one only. But there seems no reason to suppose that Nature, who has given us endless examples of her love for multiform expression, has made any such convenient arrangement ; it is quite possible that there is some basis for more methods of domification than one. The author, certainly, has spent many hours in the careful examination of horoscopes with a view to reaching a definite conclusion and nothing would give him greater pleasure than to be able to assure those who place some value upon his experience that one system is right, and one only. But to make such an affirmation with inadequate grounds would be by no means truly scientific. Far better to confess one's difficulties and perplexities.

That the passage of planets to the Campanus cusps by apparent motion (i.e., in the " progressed horoscope ") produces powerful and appropriate results, is regarded by him as undeniable. But whilst this justifies confidence in the system in this respect, it does not give the student the right to declare that the passage of bodies to cusps calculated by other methods will produce nothing at all, until he has carefully examined well-authenticated cases, with negative results.

As a purely practical measure, the author would suggest the erection of a horoscope that is to be judged by the equatorial method, but the presence of bodies on Campanus cusps, *either radical or progressed*, must be carefully noted. For, whether noted or not, they will make themselves felt.

Cases in point are Nos. 15, 16 and 17 in the writer's *Astrology of Accidents*. All these are cases or road-accidents resulting in death.

In No. 15 it is evident that the natal opposition of Mercury to Saturn was on, or very near, the cusps 3–9 at the time of death.

In No. 16 Uranus had come to opposition cusp 3.

In No. 17 Pluto, in Gemini and much afflicted, had come to the same position.

In No. 3 (boy drowned in river) it will be found that the progressed 8th cusp has reached the square of Moon opposition Mars, the latter in Scorpio.

Other cases yield equally cogent results.*

It is doubtful, in my opinion, whether either Placidus or Regiomontanus could produce results such as these. At all events, I am not aware that their advocates have as yet done so.

One of the most serious consequences of our present uncertainty as to house division is that we cannot attack the problem of the true values of the houses themselves, as conceptions, with any confidence. In particular, it is obvious that statistical methods cannot be applied to them. Indeed this is always difficult (except with the Ptolemaic or Poli-Equatorial systems) because of the differences in the " size " of the various houses and the tendency for those that lie along the horizon, both above and

---

*The Swiss maps in this work obtained from the late K. E. Krafft, are rather doubtful in regard to exactitude of time, since Continental astrologers appear often to use local time without drawing attention to their practice in so doing.

below, to be much " larger " than those that flank the meridian. It is true that in the Campanus system all houses have the same dimensions at all times ; but the arcs of the ecliptic which they contain very enormously.

We pass now to another consideration.

At the very basis of our methods of house division it would seem that there is an anomaly.

The sun (and other bodies) moves clockwise in its durnal apparent motion, but anti-clockwise in its annual passage through the zodiac.

Ought we not then, if we are to regard domification as a strictly mundane matter, to number our houses from the nadir, where the day begins, and in a clockwise sense, instead of doing so in the same sense as the signs, attributing to them also meanings analogous with those of the signs ?

It will easily be seen that our present procedure produces strange results. The cusp of the 10th, where the Sun reaches its maximum diurnal strength, is held to correspond with 0° Capricorn, where it is at its weakest point in the course of its yearly journey through the zodiac. And it is at its strongest in 0° Cancer, which is held to correspond with the nadir, where it is at its weakest in its daily apparent movement.

Again, the 12th house is held to correspond with Pisces and, therefore, is said to rule limitation, self-undoing, imprisonment, betrayal, secret enemies, and so forth. Yet it is the sector wherein the Sun and planets come into full sight after the obscuration of the night !

One might speculate as to this contradiction. Does it symbolise the conflict between Spirit and the world ?

If so, one may be cheered by the fact that, by and large, our usual interpretation *does work*, which seems to prove the *overriding importance of the zodiacal idea* and to imply that the " purely mundane " conception of the houses is a false, or rather a subordinate point of view.

By either account one would expect the *First House* to be a strong one, for its cusp is on the horizon where the celestial bodies come into sight and may certainly be assumed to exert great force.

It is said to rule the personal self, having much significance in respect of character, and also to affect the health and physical appearance. These beliefs are hardly in doubt. What has apparently never been answered is why this sector should have to do with health when that aspect of man's life is said to fall specifically under the 6th house, and what the difference is, if any, between the health-values of these two ? If, for example, a man has a bad Saturn exactly rising and a good Jupiter on cusp 6, is his bodily condition good, bad or mixed ? The 8th, too, has a health-value.

The writer's view is that the 1st house has a great deal to do with health and the 6th less than is supposed, and he would refer to Lord Tennyson's geniture given above, in which Venus rising and the Lights in sextile seem to have quite overcome the malefics in the 6th, so far as health went.

By the " purely mundane " conception the ascendant becomes the cusp of the 4th house and this may perhaps indicate that the values usually ascribed to the 1st house are inherited rather than acquired. *Note that in this way of looking at the houses (i.e., starting from the nadir and going clockwise) the 4th house begins at the ascendant and covers the area usually attributed to the 12th.*

The *Second House* is said to govern one's possessions and more especially one's private property. It has been aptly said that one's banking account is known only to oneself and to bank officials who are pledged to keep it secret, whereas the bequests that come under the 8th are set forth in wills that are open to inspection by anyone willing to pay a small fee.

Here the difficulty seems to be that Saturn has reference, more than any other horoscopic factor, to one's attitude towards property and ownership, yet it has no traditional affinity with the 2nd house.

Psychologically the author would say that the 2nd has much to do with one's contentment and ability to enjoy life. George Eliott (if her birth-time has been correctly stated) had a satellitium in Sagittarius and the 2nd house and her life was disturbed by religious and philosophical doubts and difficulties ; it is not known to the writer if she had any special attitude towards money.

From the mundane point of view this would also be the second sector and might be taken as roughly covering the years of life from seven to fourteen, including those school-days which are popularly supposed (in retrospect) to be the happiest of one's life.

The *Third House* has much to tell of the mental activities and of the actual mental ability of the native, being in this respect at least as important as Mercury. It rules all ways and means of intercommunication and is said to indicate the brethren.   Actually this last seems somewhat doubtful; the 4th house has a general rulership over the Family and the significators both of children and of brethren are often found therein.

Considered from the mundane standpoint it will be related to infancy and this agrees well enough with the traditional attributions. For the chief occupation of that stage of life is learning to talk and to walk, both 3rd house matters. From this angle, too, the nadir is the cusp of the 1st house and might be said to have personal value during the first quarter of life. That is to say, it might indicate the native's disposition during the first twenty-one years.

The *Fourth House* rules home and family and in the west

it is said to signify the father, although it is the house of the Moon by essential rulership. It is very doubtful whether this rule has much value, at least in natal astrology. The father, insofar as he and his affairs and character affect the native, is better studied through the Sun and Saturn and their aspects. Thus, George V. had Sun going to major contracts of Jupiter and Saturn and his father had Sagittarius rising and Saturn just below the ascendant. Similarly, his eldest son had Sun square Mars, his own ruler.

As we have said above, this house has a wide value in respect of the family, yet, paradoxically, it is said to rule the end of life when one's elders have often died and one's children may be dispersed. Certainly bodies on the nadir often affect health, and aspects formed by it may indicate death. By Mundane symbology one would expect the area of the 4th house to rule the end of life, for from this point of view it is the last house. But its cusp would not be the nadir, but that upon the traditional 5th, for the reasons we have explained.

Psychologically it probably rules the depth and sincerity of the affections, especially those arising from family ties.

The *Fifth House* is a great creative factor, on the physical level ruling the children but also concerned with literary and artistic creation when the appropriate planets are placed in it.

In the normal type of map it stands for the pleasures and describes the fields in which the native seeks enjoyment and recreation, so that a certain type of affliction here will point to sensual pursuits and a low standard of morality, which sacrifices too much to pleasure. Immorality is especially apt to arise when the pleasure-seeking planets, of which Jupiter is probably the worst addict, are involved.

Gambling and all games of hazard are placed under the 5th house.

Thus it would not be too much to postulate that the term " the house of self-undoing " is much more applicable to this sector than to the maligned 12th house, which more often points to trouble through other people. Those who have ruined themselves through self-indulgence and recklessness, rather than by errors of judgment, will usually show in their nativities an involvement of the 5th house in affliction.

From the pure mundane point of view it would seem that the entire north-west quadrant indicates an *obscuration and a decline in power*, since bodies therein are both beneath the earth and sinking towards the nadir.

It is held to signify the native's offspring, through correspondence with Leo and the Sun and this certainly often holds good. Later, however, we shall refer to this matter again in relation to another house.

The *Sixth House* is held to rule one's work, especially that which is of a routine nature with an element of drudgery, one's servants and social inferiors, and one's health, these being obviously based on the analogy with Virgo.

It has a very strong (but apparently overlooked) relation with the disposition, especially one's moods, temper and manners. Just as we have suggested that the 1st has much more value in terms of the health than this house, so we now suggest that the 6th often overrides the ascendant, to some extent, in respect of temperament. The natus of Tennyson is a case in point ; he had Venus rising in Gemini but this did not prevent his demeanour in society often being gruff and ungracious ; and this we attribute to the malefics which (by any count) are to be found in the 6th. Furthermore, Venus rising did not render him by any means always cheerful and light-hearted. In another case known to us Mars afflicted in the 6th gave a most violent temper, and Uranus in the 6th, though in trine to the same planet, appears to have produced a similar propensity in Henry VIII. On the other hand, Venus here denotes a placid disposition and Jupiter a cheery or philosophical outlook.

The rulership over servants and employees generally and over one's own work seems well established, the latter ascription contrasting with the dominion of the 5th over pleasure, holidays and " spare time."

The *Seventh House* is entitled to hold its traditional rulership over marriage and all other partnerships and over one's public appearances and relations with the public. It leads, in fact, to personal publicity. It is usually regarded as a favourable emplacement for good planets, but strength here often means weakness in the purely personal expression of the 1st house. It gives the sort of temperament that is more at home on the platform than in private circumstances and inclines to the playing of a part in public. The fate, too, is often in the hands of others.

Planets actually setting affect by opposition the health,* and in the case of malefics the results are often severe ; whether benefics on the descendant are to be accounted good for the 7th or evil because of their opposition to the 1st, is a moot-point. Probably the results will be mixed.

Married happiness seems to depend more upon Venus than upon the 7th and even evil planets in this house are not by any means incompatible with connubial felicity, though they will probably introduce material difficulties, such as finance or ill-health.

The *Eighth House* is said to rule the goods of the dead, and death itself, though some modern writers have limited this to violent deaths and decease from unnatural causes.

---

*Bodies exactly on cusps seem more often to affect the opposed house than the one in which they are.

PROBLEMS OF THE HOUSES

It is also stated to have much to do with spiritualism and necromancy inasmuch as these pursuits are connected with the afterdeath condition.

However, it has a general application to physical condition and in this respect is more important than the 6th. Perhaps it has to do with the state, healthy or otherwise, of the large aqueous content of the body, the 6th being rather concerned with the tissues, and the ascendant with the vital powers.

Certainly it has much to do with the tendency to thinness or obesity, as the case may be, and the presence of the Moon, Jupiter or Neptune in this sector, or a close aspect to the cusp from them, inclines to stoutness, whilst Saturn has a contrary effect. One of the leanest persons known to the writer has Jupiter precisely rising (in Virgo) but Saturn is close to the 8th cusp.

Again, it resembles the 6th in influencing the moods and general temperament, strong malefic configurations being dangerous in point of character, as may be seen in the case of Mussolini and Hitler, whose respective Gemini and Taurus groupings may be considered, for the reasons we have given, to affect the 8th cusp even if they are actually in the 7th house.

The 8th is commonly tenanted in the maps of surgeons, doctors and nurses, soldiers and sailors, detectives, inspectors of all kinds (but especially those connected with sanitation) and mediums. Butchers and undertakers can probably be included.

From the mundane point of view it will roughly rule the period from 49 to 56, when, as a rule, one has attained, or failed to attain, a position in life and begins to taste the fruits, sweet or bitter, of the years of vigour and endeavour. There is, normally, a decline in outer activity and either a turning to the inner life or a general " slackening off." However, a forceful nativity will pass through this epoch and remain active, in some field, to the end.

The *Ninth House* stands at the apex of the fiery houses. For it is surely legitimate (though unusual) to attribute not only meanings to the houses in correspondence with the signs, but also elemental characteristics.

As such, it is the summit of aspiration and the outgoing and upward-tending emotions. It is said to rule law, foreign countries and travel therein, and religion. We have touched on these matters in speaking of Sagittarius. Certainly the two latter attributions should stand ; law is perhaps a little less simple a matter. Several jurists and judges appear in *One Thousand and One* and curiously enough there does not seem to be a single body in the 9th house in any of them.

It is probably the house of the *conscience* insofar as this is regarded as an implanted sense of right and wrong and not simply the result of training in social taboos, which is a Saturnian-lunar matter, though, even from the latter point of view, it might affect the degree to which the individual is receptive to such training. If we accept Shelley as an example of conscience—he forwent an inheritance of £10,000 a year as a protest against primogeniture—we find that he had, by the Equatorial system, Mercury in the 9th in Virgo in close trine to Saturn in the firm sign Taurus. In Mussolini's case it is true that, by this system, both benefics are in the 9th, but its ruler (which is also their dispositrix) is terribly afflicted. In Hitler's case its ruler Mercury is opposed to Uranus, showing not so much absence of conscience as a perverted one.

It would probably be correct to regard this house as being normally a good one, partaking in some degree of the exalted nature of the 10th and potentially controlling and guiding the primitive outrush of the 1st and the pleasure-seeking propensity of the 5th.

However, if we use the Equatorial method we shall find that it is often held by malefics in criminal horoscopes, which may be taken as betokening both their criminality and their sufferings at the hands of the law. Mars would tend to a violent and resentful nature ; Saturn to one that is avaricious and envious.

The *Tenth House* represents on the positive side the status and authority of the native, and, on the negative, his masters and those who exercise control over him. Interiorly it stands for his ambitions on the positive side, and on the negative for his self-respect and sense of responsibility.

The midheaven marks the highest elevation above the horizon which each body reaches in the course of its diurnal arc, along which it passes from rising to setting. On the other hand, the point in square to the ascending degree, which is the 10th cusp by the Ptolemaic system, marks the most elevated point, at any given moment, of the semicircle of the ecliptic which is then above the horizon. The distinction, perplexing to the beginner, is easily grasped by means of a celestial globe. In practice, it will be seen that both points have a similar significance and one that is analogous to the point of Capricorn.

Here we may recall the anomaly which we have indicated above : the Sun, diurnally, is strongest on the 10th cusp and yet it is weakest, zodiacally speaking, in 0° Capricorn. The opposition between Christmas and midday is obvious. The festival celebrates the rebirth of the sun ; the mid-day hour marks its greatest splendour, its pinnacle of glory.

And the contradiction appears in practical form. The Moon is held to rule the 4th house essentially, and rightly so ; yet the Moon has a liking for publicity. One need only study the maps of a few editors for proof of this. On the other hand, Saturn is the natural lord of the 10th, and yet its bent is not towards publicity; it has an element of reserve.

Thus in a sense the 10th has some natural affinity not only with Saturn but with the Moon. In another sense, all bodies are extremely strong when on the meridian or when in square to the ascendant from elevation, for the two distinct reasons given above.

It is at these points that the not-self confronts the self from elevation ; and fortunate are those for whom they hold no adverse stress, such as a square to a rising planet.

Symbolically, an opposition to the 1st from the 7th shows an enemy met on equal terms, but the square from the southern meridian represents one who comes as a would-be master, just as the square from the 4th is the enemy within the gates, i.e., as a rule, a psychological weakness.

From the mundane point of view the 10th becomes the 6th house, with its cusp at the 11th. And thus we get a good reason why the 10th shows one's vocation and one's success in that direction, as well as disappointment and drudgery.

The *Eleventh House* is commonly regarded as a generally fortunate one ; it is the *agathos daimon*, or good angel, of the Greeks, who doubtless took this conception from the Chaldeans. We attribute to it our wishes and aspirations, which are the more spiritual aspect of the pleasures of the 5th, and our friends, whom we choose, as we cannot choose our children, for their congeniality with ourselves. On the whole, it is a house about which our writers have said little, perhaps because friendship does not play as great a part in Anglo-Saxon life as in that of some other nations, past and present. Or, at all events, we talk of it less.

But this house is important. It substands the 10th, as the 2nd substands the 1st, building up the native's success and public status through his friendly associations and inspiring him through its aspirational activity.   Strong planets placed here bring him upward, as they pass to the 10th house and the meridian, and conversely with weak ones ; the 10th is largely the fruit of the 11th. Indeed, it sometimes seems as if a good 11th will overcome an afflicted 10th as the life progresses.

It is probable that it has much to do with all occupations that involve the native's association with others, on more or less equal terms and *en masse* rather than individually. As, for example, that of the politician.

The *Twelfth House*, as we have remarked, offers a sharp contrast between the two views of the houses which we have put forward.   For, as corresponding with Pisces, it has a traditionally gloomy reputation, and was the Evil Angel of the Greeks. That this is true enough, up to a point seems undeniable. It has an aspect of confinement and limitation, as is evidenced by the horoscopes of prisoners of war, which usually show bodies afflicted in the 12th. In this sense it recalls Saturn, as well as Neptune, for who knew more of the " ring pass not " associated with the former planet, than these men ? Afflicted bodies in the 12th show disappointment and frustation, and sorrow not only on one's own behalf, but very frequently for others. They draw sorrowful conditions around the native like magnets.

Generally it is true to say that the Saturnian frustrations and inhibitions are of a more definite kind, and they are often associated with matters of finance or are connected with the government or with those in authority over one. Whereas the 12th house afflicts through sickness, either one's own or that of others, or general misfortunes.

Yet one cannot always distinguish these classes easily. In the case of a man who had Sun opposed to Saturn, 3rd to 9th, there was a life-long inhibition of movement due to a tubercular foot, with much illness and pain, whilst in the case of another who had malefics in Pisces in the 12th, very similar conditions arose : the ailment was different but the effects were alike.

Perhaps it would be safe to say that the *psychological reactions* would usually be different, the Saturn affliction inclining to a Stoic endurance and the Piscean to a more sympathetic attitude towards others, and, if one may put it so, to oneself, Saturn is apt to take misfortune as a fact in life and get on with it, but to the Piscean (and in this term we include those largely under the 12th house) it is not only an affliction, but also a human problem.

One must, however, also consider this house when it is not afflicted, for a gloomy picture can be painted of any of the twelve if we regard it only in its negative aspect. It is, from the mundane point of view, the house of the Risen Sun, and, as such, one would expect it to connote not obscuration, but exactly the reverse. Except that it would stand not for full manifestation, but for the first degree of manifestation, man so to speak in the attainment of his majority, the period from twenty-one to twenty-eight years.

It is the opinion of most astrologers that strong bodies in the 12th, as they pass into the 11th and 10th houses, will bring good fortune and a blossoming forth at maturity, though it is probable that the 12th is not so good in this respect as the 11th, if only because the good effects will come later and there will be less time to develop them. Also, the native with a powerful 12th house influence is seldom personally ambitious ; he will probably retain throughout life a certain tendency towards seclusion, and his occupations will often be such as do not bring him greatly before the public. Your true 12th-house person is usually a poor and unwilling mixer unless he is in an entirely congenial company. Alan Leo was a poor lecturer and was courteous rather than expansive in social life.

Vivian Robson, with Moon conjoined to Saturn in the 12th, was a typical recluse.

It is a curious fact that this house often has a relation to one's eldest child, perhaps because, in a physical sense, it carries on one's own life, which expires in this sector. I do not think this point has ever before been noted but a study of well-authenticated nativities will confirm it, especially if the Campanus method of domification be employed, though there are of course frequent exceptions.

Thus Queen Victoria had Pisces on cusp 12 and her eldest child had that sign rising. King Edward VII had Mercury there, and the Duke of Clarence was born under Virgo. George V had the end of Capricorn on the 12th, and the Duke of Windsor was born under the beginning of the next sign.

INDEX

182

184

186

Better books make better astrologers.
Here are some of our other titles:

AstroAmerica's Daily Ephemeris, 2010-2020
AstroAmerica's Daily Ephemeris, 2000-2020
 - both for Midnight. Compiled & formatted by David R. Roell

Al Biruni
**The Book of Instructions in the Elements of the Art of
 Astrology**, *1029 AD, translated by R. Ramsay Wright*

Derek Appleby
Horary Astrology: The Art of Astrological Divination

E. H. Bailey
The Prenatal Epoch

Joseph Blagrave
Astrological Practice of Physick

C.E.O. Carter
The Astrology of Accidents
An Encyclopaedia of Psychological Astrology
The Principles of Astrology, *Intermediate no. 1*
Some Principles of Horoscopic Delineation, *Intermediate no. 2*
Symbolic Directions in Modern Astrology

Charubel & Sepharial
Degrees of the Zodiac Symbolized, *1898*

Nicholas Culpeper
**Astrological Judgement of Diseases from the Decumbiture of
 the Sick**, *1655, and,* **Urinalia**, *1658*

Dorotheus of Sidon
Carmen Astrologicum, *c. 50 AD, translated by David Pingree*

Nicholas deVore
Encyclopedia of Astrology

Firmicus Maternus
Ancient Astrology Theory & Practice: Matheseos Libri VIII,
c. 350 AD, translated by Jean Rhys Bram

William Lilly
Christian Astrology, books 1 & 2, *1647*
 The Introduction to Astrology, Resolution of all manner of questions.
Christian Astrology, book 3, *1647*
 Easie and plaine method teaching how to judge upon nativities.

CPSIA information can be obtained at www.ICGtesting.com
Printed in the USA
BVOW08s1133300815

415744BV00001B/16/P